I0066751

The Warrior Mom's Guide to ZBB & Cash Stuffing

Zero-Based Budgeting & Cash Envelope Systems for
Sick-Day Survival

Shaundra M. G. Harris

The Warrior Mom's Guide to ZBB & Cash Stuffing

Zero-Based Budgeting & Cash Envelope Systems for
Sick-Day Survival

Shaundra M. G. Harris

Shaun The Mom Publishing

© 2025 Shaundra M. G. Harris.

All rights reserved.

Paperback ISBN: 978-1-969446-07-8

Hardback ISBN: 978-1-969446-17-7

First Edition

No part of this publication may be reproduced, stored in a retrieval system, or transmitted in any form without written permission from the author, except by reviewers or educators using brief quotations with proper citation.

Publisher Shaun The Mom Publishing

Printed in the United States.

www.shaunthemom.com

www.warriormomacademy.com

Disclaimer

This book is intended for informational and inspirational purposes only. The content reflects the personal experiences, opinions, and insights of the author and should not be considered a substitute for professional medical, legal, financial, educational, therapeutic, or spiritual advice.

While the author shares tools, tips, and resources that have been personally helpful, every situation is unique. Readers are encouraged to consult with qualified professionals before making decisions regarding health, finances, homeschooling, parenting, estate planning, or other matters discussed in this book.

Some links or references provided may be affiliate links. This means the author may receive a small commission at no extra cost to you if you choose to purchase through those links. These recommendations are made in good faith and only include resources the author personally uses or believes may be helpful.

Any printable templates, checklists, or workbook materials included are for personal use only and may not be distributed, sold, or used commercially without written permission from the author.

The author and publisher expressly disclaim any liability arising directly or indirectly from the use or misuse of any information, tools, or resources included in this book

-To the Warrior Moms who fight daily battles with grace, strength, and relentless hope—especially those navigating chronic illness and financial challenges alone.

May this book empower you to reclaim your finances, your peace, and your future. You are seen, you are valued, and you are never alone.

-To my children Aoki, Layla, Jayden, and Nia.

Welcome to the Warrior Mom Academy

Welcome, Warrior Mom.

You've arrived in a space made just for you—a community of fierce, loving mothers who refuse to let chronic illness or financial hardship define their story.

The Warrior Mom Academy is where we find clarity amidst chaos, where budgeting becomes a tool of empowerment, not stress.

Here, we celebrate every small win and share the wisdom of real moms who have walked this path.

This guide is more than numbers and envelopes— it's a roadmap to financial freedom, peace of mind, and joy in the journey.

Take what you need, leave what you don't, and know that I am with you every step of the way.

Welcome to your tribe.

Welcome home.

— Shaun

Table of Contents

THE WARRIOR MOM GUIDES

Introduction

A Letter to the Reader: You Are Not Alone

Dear Warrior Mom,

If you're holding this book, chances are you're juggling a lot—motherhood, chronic illness, and the weight of managing tight finances all at once. I see you. I hear you. And more importantly, I want you to know you are not alone.

For years, I struggled with the overwhelm of trying to stretch every dollar while navigating the unpredictable nature of chronic illness. Some days, it felt like the finances were controlling me—like I was always behind, always catching up, always exhausted.

But something shifted when I discovered zero-based budgeting and cash stuffing—not just as budgeting methods, but as tools of empowerment.

Suddenly, I could tell every dollar where to go instead of wondering where my money disappeared. I could create boundaries for my spending that honored my health and my family's needs. I began to see progress, no matter how small, and with it, hope.

This book is my way of sharing that breakthrough with you. It's a guide written specifically for single moms like us who face the unique challenges of chronic illness, low or fixed income, and the emotional rollercoaster of trying to build financial stability.

Here, you'll find practical steps, gentle encouragement, real stories from moms who've been there, and tools designed to work with your energy, not against it.

This isn't about perfection or one-size-fits-all budgeting.

It's about creating a plan that fits your life, honors your limitations, and leads you toward peace of mind.

You deserve to take control of your finances, so they don't control you.

So, take a deep breath, Mama.

Let's walk this path together—one dollar at a time.

With hope and solidarity,

Shaun

My Financial Journey with Sickle Cell Anemia

Let's get into it.

When I was about 15 and a half, I started dating this older guy. He was nice to me and after some family drama we agreed we move in together. Back then, I was much younger, and to say I was healthier is an understatement. I was able to work without getting sick or having a major crisis.

I worked a lot—sometimes two jobs at a time— because one of the ways he controlled me was financially. Once he started to treat me poorly, I thought of ways to improve my situation, but I had nothing and nowhere to go.

As I was still a minor and he was an adult, everything was in his name and under his control. He controlled the finances, the car I didn't even have a license of course, because I was living with him, doing everything from cooking and cleaning to working, all for nothing but a roof over my head.

Sounds rough, right? Well, sarcasm aside, what do you call it when you're stuck with someone who treats you poorly and uses money as a means of control? He'd ask for my paycheck on payday, take 75% of it for "our needs," and leave me with just enough to survive.

Eventually, I caught on. I realized what he was doing—keeping me financially limited. So, I made a plan. I started stacking my money and saving for me and my new baby . I started working at a bank as a teller, I loved it.

That was a turning point in my life. I was introduced to a whole new world of money. As a teller, I got to see firsthand how wealthy people built their fortunes through dividends, stocks, businesses, and investments. It was amazing to witness how they set up generational wealth.

Around the same time, I started watching "The Suze Orman Show", and let me tell you—it was pure gold. I learned a lot, and deep down, I wanted to have the kind of money problems people called in about. I wanted to call Suze and ask, "How do I invest my millions into generational wealth?" I was ready for all the financial smoke.

I learned more and more, working for the bank. While watching and doing the things my peers were telling me my bank account grew. I was training to be a lead teller and I eventually wanted to become a personal banker. But life happened. My then first ex-not-husband convinced me to quit the bank job, and after draining my savings, I ended up working at a local grocery store.

My older brother suggested working with him at a retail store across the lot, where I could make more money and they had a night shift, I could work while my baby was sleeping. Oh yeah, I had, had a baby. So, the mission to get money was top priority.

Shortly After starting, I decided to officially leave my abusive relationship and start fresh with my daughter. We didn't have anything except a couch that I purchased for $50 worth of food stamps. Shout out my neighbor Ms. Goldsmith. But we were gonna be okay. I started saving and planning.

A few months into working, I met my second not-husband. The man who I would later be with for over 12 years. In the beginning things seemed to be going good in our relationship. So, about a year into it we decided to have a baby, and while the pregnancy was already rocky, the birth went from bad to worse.

While pregnant I was informed my maternity leave was approved, but due to a waiting period delay I wouldn't qualify for leave with pay. In a panic I started working more hours to save up to be able to stay home with the baby.

The father said he would get two jobs if he had to but wasn't able to do so. The stress from work, my health crises, and trying to manage being a mother was overwhelming. The situation worsened when I found out that I wouldn't qualify for maternity pay, which I was counting on. My stress led to one of the worst sickle cell crises of my life, resulting in a premature labor, intubation and induced coma for a few days.

So, I worked myself into a Sickle Cell Crises. No surprise there. It landed me in the hospital for weeks. I ended up missing the only baby shower ever held for me.

They tried to control the crisis with blood transfusions, hydration and various medications with little to no result. Things got bad an a emergency caesarean was ordered.

I had to go through a difficult C-section, followed by pulmonary edema and internal bleeding. The stress from everything—my finances, my relationship, and my health—landed me in the hospital. Being placed in an induced coma on a ventilator for three days, it was a wake-up call. But I didn't answer.

I returned to work with the same mindset. It was still time to get to this money. That experience taught me still, that no one was coming to save me. It was time for me to grab the ladder.

I went from overnight stock associate to a guest service representative, to front end team leader, to senior team leader. The money was starting to flow, and I was doing my best to manage it. Our life started improving and I found us a house to rent. I also transferred to another retail location closer to our new home.

I thought maybe a better quality of life, would change my circumstances. Show my family what was possible. Life got better for a while, but problems started to arise. While lies and infidelities were always an issue, and we were always "working thru it". His money habits like his flesh were weak, and I was trying to be saved and savvy. It was hard.

To make things worse, my sister became critically ill, and I was named her guardian and advocate. She was pregnant and dealing with a sickle cell crisis that required airlifting her to a hospital over an hour away.

I was juggling caring for her, managing my family, working a retail job, and keeping everything afloat. Eventually, I lost that job, and the stress only grew. Since I was already home, we decided to try the stay-at-home mom thing. After all, our family was expanding faster than we expected.

So, I couldn't give up. I started working on our finances. My guy and I researched ways to build credit, buy property, and improve our financial situation. He started working at a good company, one that paid decently and allowed me to build.

Things seemed like they were on track I even started budgeting and using couponing. After a few months of savvy money management, we had about $2,000 saved up. But there was a huge turning point.

He said something that triggered a change in me. When I showed him our savings and started suggesting how we could use it wisely, he said,

"How are you spending my money?"

That was it. I realized that if I was going to make this work, I had to do it on my own. He clearly did not see us as partners or team, nor did he have our family's best interest at heart.

My determination to succeed financially was stronger than ever. And that's when I got serious about learning how to build wealth, just like the rich folks I'd been studying.

At this point, I was obsessed with learning how to build wealth and transfer it to future generations. But life wasn't going to make it easy. My health worsened again, and I found myself in a constant battle with my finances, my health, and my relationship.

As things got worse, I had to make some hard decisions. I realized I had to leave my partner because he wasn't contributing to our financial or emotional stability. I was holding it all together, and I realized that if I had to go through this alone, I might as well be alone.

But then life threw another curveball. My daughter got into a car accident while I was recovering from health issues, and my car insurance didn't cover it. It added to the financial burden, and I was left dealing with the aftermath of a total loss and voluntary surrender. Instead of a repossession I did a MEpossession. They didn't come take truck; I gave it back. But on your credit report it affects it the same if the balance is not paid, so there's that blip.

By 2023, I was facing bankruptcy, with over $140,000 in debt. I didn't have enough food to feed my kids and pay my bills. I was on the verge of losing everything and begin speaking with lawyers. But during this time, I heard a piece of advice from Dave Ramsey that changed my life:

"First, feed your babies."

That was all I needed to hear. He was giving advice to a caller in my same shoes. She was trying to feed her children and meet minimum payments and often couldn't do both. Dave said forget them bills and feed them kids. First and always. Now I'm adding on here, but you get it.

I stopped relying on old financial strategies that weren't working and adopted a new, simple approach. I created a budget that was realistic for my situation. I started focusing on my family's needs first. I paid what I could with what I had, and I made plans to pay the rest later.

I called this my "Broke Budget." It wasn't pretty, but it was effective. I focused on feeding my family, taking care of my basic needs, and slowly rebuilding my financial life. I stopped stressing about what I couldn't control and started focusing on the essentials.

I also the power of zero-based budgeting. Every dollar had a purpose. I only spent what was allocated for each category. And I started teaching my kids about budgeting too. They had their own funds from allowance to make special purchases.

Through all of this, I learned the importance of prayer and planning. I prayed for guidance, strength, and provision, and I created a plan that was simple and practical.

Today, I am a self-published author, and my income has grown in ways I never thought possible. I went from barely making ends meet to living a life that's a testament to the power of persistence, prayer, and financial discipline.

I'm living proof that with God, all things are possible.

If I can make it out of poverty and rebuild my life, so can you. Trust the process, make a plan, and never give up.

Why This Book?

Life as a single mom with a chronic illness is anything but simple.

You're balancing fatigue, medical appointments, parenting, and bills—often all at the same time.

Most traditional budgeting advice doesn't take these unique challenges into account.

That's why this book was created specifically for you: to help build a financial system that honors your energy, your reality, and your goals.

Whether you're living on a tight or fixed income, this guide offers practical, realistic tools that empower you to take control of your money without burning out.

You'll find strategies tailored for the unpredictability of chronic illness, alongside encouragement and resources that remind you

—you are not alone in this journey.

How to Use This Book

This book is designed to meet you where you are—whether you're just beginning to think about budgeting or have tried many times before.

It's not about perfection or strict rules; it's about creating a flexible, sustainable system that fits your life and respects your limits.

- Read at your own pace. Each chapter is a step forward, but you can skip around to what feels most urgent.
- Use the tools and templates. They're designed for low-energy days and can be adapted to your needs.
- Reflect often. Take time to journal or think through your feelings about money—it's part of healing your financial story.
- Come back when you need a boost. This book is a companion, not a one-time read.

Your financial breakthrough doesn't have to be perfect or fast—it just has to be real and sustainable for you.

Understanding the Challenges of Budgeting with Chronic Illness

Living with a chronic illness, such as sickle cell anemia, is not just a physical challenge; it's an emotional and financial one as well.

As a mother, you may find yourself balancing the demands of raising children while managing the unpredictable and often expensive nature of chronic health conditions.

The financial strain can feel overwhelming, especially when you add in the cost of healthcare, medications, treatments, and the occasional emergency medical situation.

In this section, we'll explore some of the unique challenges that single mothers with chronic illnesses face when it comes to budgeting and managing finances.

The Emotional and Physical Toll of Chronic Illness

Chronic illnesses, like sickle cell anemia, can cause periods of high pain, fatigue, and medical appointments, all of which disrupt your daily life and often prevent you from working as much as you would like to.

This can result in inconsistent income, making budgeting more difficult. It's not just the financial strain that weighs heavily on your shoulders- there's also the emotional burden of constantly managing your health while ensuring your family has everything it needs.

When you experience flare-ups, fatigue, or other debilitating symptoms, managing your health becomes the priority, which can make it challenging to focus on your finances. This can lead to unintentional financial neglect, missed bills, or impulse spending to alleviate stress.

These emotional reactions to financial stress are natural but need to be managed in a way that doesn't undermine your long-term financial stability.

Unpredictable Medical Expenses

A significant aspect of budgeting with chronic illness is anticipating medical costs. Unlike a healthy person who may only visit the doctor a few times a year, chronic illness often requires frequent check-ups, prescriptions, therapies, and sometimes emergency care.

These expenses can add up quickly and without warning. Some of the common medical costs include:

- Doctor's appointments and specialist visits
- Medications and prescriptions
- Lab work and diagnostic tests
- Hospital stays and emergency room visits
- Physical therapy and alternative treatments

Many people with chronic illnesses also face the challenge of medications that may not be covered by insurance or may require out-of-pocket payments. This adds another layer of unpredictability to your finances, making it difficult to plan for emergencies or future expenses.

Dealing with Inconsistent or Limited Income

As a single mother with a chronic illness, your income may fluctuate depending on your ability to work.

On good days, you might be able to work full-time or part-time, but on days when your illness flares up, it may be difficult to work at all.

Even if you have a steady income, your health might still limit the number of hours you can work, causing an income gap that's hard to predict.

Here are a few ways this might play out:

Reduced working hours:

If you're not able to work full-time due to fatigue, doctor's visits, or other symptoms, your monthly income may be inconsistent.

Frequent absences from work:

Unforeseen sick days or hospital visits might lead to missed wages, and for some, there may be no paid leave or sick time.

Disability benefits:

Depending on your situation, you may qualify for government assistance programs, such as Social Security Disability Insurance (SSDI) or Supplemental Security Income (SSI), but navigating these applications can be time-consuming and emotionally draining.

I waited close to two years for my approval, and it was a very stressful time.

The Pressure of Parenting Alone

As a single mother, you bear the full responsibility of caring for your children while managing your own health needs.

This can feel like a juggling act, where every decision counts and every expense feels high stakes. Add to this the emotional toll of raising children alone while trying to keep things financially stable, and it's no wonder that many single mothers in this situation feel overwhelmed.

Financial stress can be particularly taxing on your mental health, which, in turn, affects your ability to make sound financial decisions.

When you're juggling the role of a parent, health advocate, and primary breadwinner, it's easy to let certain tasks slide, like tracking spending or planning for future needs.

How This Affects Your Financial Mindset

Understanding these challenges helps to frame how financial decisions are made. If you have been living with chronic illness for some time, you may have developed coping strategies to manage financial stress.

Some of these strategies may work well, but others may unintentionally contribute to your stress. For instance, you may find yourself "just getting by" without fully thinking through the long-term implications of your financial choices.

The good news is that once you understand how chronic illness affects your finances, you can begin to make intentional decisions that serve both your immediate needs and long-term goals.

Budgeting doesn't have to feel like an extra stressor- it can actually help reduce financial anxiety by providing you with a roadmap and structure.

Empathy and Action: Taking the First Step Toward Financial Control

In this book, you will learn practical strategies to take control of your finances, even amidst the unpredictability that comes with living with chronic illness. While the journey may seem daunting, you're not alone.

Countless other single mothers are in similar situations and have successfully managed their finances by utilizing a variety of techniques such as zero-based budgeting, cash stuffing, and living below their means.

Each chapter will give you the tools to:

- Establish a sustainable budget that accommodates your unique needs
- Prepare for unexpected medical expenses
- Stay financially resilient despite the challenges of chronic illness

By the end of this book, you'll have a clear, actionable plan to gain control over your financial situation- without feeling like you're constantly putting out fires or living paycheck to paycheck.

Next Steps: What You Can Do Right Now

Before diving into the rest of the book, take a moment to reflect on where you are financially and emotionally.

Think about the challenges you've faced and the obstacles you see ahead.

Acknowledge those feelings, but remember, with the right tools and strategies, you can begin to change your financial future.

The next step is to take control through budgeting.

Define objectives and set financial goals:

- Define short-term and long-term goals you want to achieve with your budget, like saving for a down payment on a house, paying off debt, or building an emergency fund.

- Start by understanding the goal of your budgeting. Whether it will be a monthly, quarterly, or annual budget. This helps you to understand the flow of your budget and assist in aligning the budget to specific objectives.

For example:

If you are currently living paycheck to paycheck your goal may be to not.

So, getting a handle on your "day to day" budget and creating a buffer/emergency fund may be goals.

If on a fixed income your budget plans may include: the day-to-day expenses, your month-to-month budget, and future planning for quarterly and annual expenses.

Whatever your personal financial goals and budgeting needs, ZBB will help you achieve them.

By the end of this book, you'll have a toolkit designed around you.

One that supports you in your hard days and helps you grow on your good days.

Let's get started—together.

Part I: Building Your Financial Foundation

Build a strong mindset and develop a clear picture of your current financial reality. This section introduces non-judgmental self-assessment, realistic goal-setting, and practical steps to organize finances that work with your health fluctuations.

Chapter 1: Understanding Your Financial Reality

Before you can take control of your finances, you need a clear picture of where you are right now.

This chapter gently guides you through understanding your income, spending, and debts—without shame or judgment.

Awareness is the first step to empowerment, and that's exactly where we'll begin.

Taking Inventory: Income, Expenses, and Debts

Understanding Your Income

Start by calculating your total monthly net income—the amount you actually bring home after taxes and deductions. This includes:

- Wages or salary
- Freelance or gig income
- Side hustles
- Rental income
- Child support or government assistance

Be realistic. Low-income households often deal with fluctuating income, so it's helpful to look at an average of the last 2–3 months if your income varies.

To get started:

- Gather bank statements, pay stubs, and any other income records.
- Review at least 3 months of bank activity to identify patterns.
- Make a note of income frequency (weekly, biweekly, monthly, etc.).

This step is crucial. Your income is the starting point for your budget. Everything you plan financially—saving, spending, and paying off debt—will flow from this number.

Types of Income

It's helpful to understand how you earn income, so you can plan for stability and growth.

Most people receive a combination of active and passive income.

Active Income

This is money earned through direct effort—working a job or running a business. Examples include:

- Wages, salaries, commissions
- Bonuses or tips
- Net earnings from self-employment

Active income is the most common and typically used for everyday expenses.

Passive Income

This is money earned without active daily involvement. While some passive income streams take time to build, they can lead to long-term stability.

Examples include:

- Rental income
- Dividends or interest
- Royalties or annuities
- Affiliate marketing or ad revenue (e.g., YouTube, blogs)
- Income from digital products (e.g., ebooks, courses)

Now that you understand the types of income, add up yours. You need to know what's coming in before you can tell it where to go.

Calculate and Track Your Spending

For one full month, write down everything you spend money on—no matter how small. Categorize your spending into groups like:

- Housing
- Utilities
- Groceries
- Transportation
- Entertainment

You'll need to list all your expenses—even those that don't happen every month. This gives you a full picture of where your money is going and helps identify unnecessary or harmful spending patterns.

Types of Expenses

Fixed Expenses

These are predictable and consistent—bills that are due on the same date every month:

- Rent or mortgage
- Car payments
- Insurance premiums
- Student loans
- Internet, phone bills
- Subscriptions or memberships

These should typically take up no more than 50% of your income.

Variable Expenses

These change from month to month and are often based on usage or choices:

- Groceries
- Gas or transportation
- Utilities (like electric, water)
- Entertainment
- Clothing

- Personal care (haircuts, self-care)
- Medical costs
- Repairs or services

Tips for managing variable expenses:

1. Use the envelope method (assign cash to each category).
2. Limit these to no more than 30% of your income.
3. Track and review spending weekly or monthly.

Periodic Expenses

These are expenses that happen quarterly, semi-annually, or yearly. Because they don't show up monthly, they're often forgotten until it's too late.

Examples include:

- Car registration
- Property taxes
- Insurance premiums
- Holiday or birthday costs
- Annual memberships or subscriptions

How to manage them:

1. Estimate the yearly total for each.
2. Divide by 12 to save for them monthly.
3. Use a savings account or sinking fund envelope.

Don't let these catch you off guard. Planning ahead reduces stress and keeps your budget on track.

Analyze Spending Patterns

Once you've tracked your spending, ask yourself:

1. Is this necessary?
2. Does it support my goals?
3. Can I spend less here or cut it out altogether?
4. Are there cheaper alternatives?

This is about evaluating every expense based on your priorities—not someone else's. Zero-based budgeting will challenge you to justify every dollar and reallocate it with intention.

Create Expense Categories & Prioritize Spending

Next, group your expenses into categories and rank them by priority. Here's a helpful order:

1. Essentials first – rent, food, utilities, transportation
2. Debt repayment and savings – pay off debt and build your emergency fund
3. Discretionary last – only spend on entertainment or non-essentials after essentials and goals are covered

This system makes sure your most critical needs are met, your future is protected, and your spending aligns with your values.

In Summary

Taking control of your finances starts with understanding exactly where you are.

That means:

- Knowing how much money you really have
- Understanding where it comes from
- Tracking where it goes
- Evaluating what's truly necessary
- Prioritizing what matters most

This work is powerful. It's how you reclaim financial control, even in the face of uncertainty.

Let's keep going—you've got this.

🐝 Reflection | Affirmation | Prayer | Action

Understanding Your Financial Reality

Reflection

1. How do I honestly feel about my current financial situation?
2. What patterns—emotional, circumstantial, or habitual—have shaped the way I handle money?
3. Am I carrying shame or guilt about my financial choices or past experiences?
4. What truths about my income, expenses, and spending habits have I been avoiding?

Affirmation

I am not defined by my past financial mistakes.

I face my finances with courage, clarity, and compassion.

Every dollar I track is a step toward healing and wholeness.

I am capable of creating a budget that reflects my values and supports my needs.

Prayer

God, help me to see my finances through Your eyes—not through fear or comparison.

Give me the wisdom to steward what I have well, and the strength to make necessary changes with grace.

Heal the places where lack or struggle has wounded my heart.

Let this journey toward financial clarity also be a journey of spiritual and emotional renewal. Amen.

Action

- Set aside 30–60 minutes this week to review your income and expenses.
- Track every dollar that has come in and gone out over the past 30 days.
- Highlight any categories that surprise or concern you—without judgment.
- Choose one small change you can make this week (e.g., unsubscribe from an unused service, pack lunch twice, start a spending log).
- Celebrate this step. Awareness is progress. You're moving forward.

Chapter 2: Zero-Based Budgeting 101

"You don't need more money—you need a better plan for what you already have."

Welcome to one of the most empowering financial strategies out there: zero-based budgeting (ZBB).

In this chapter, you'll learn how it works, why it's a game changer—especially for low-income households—and how to use it to finally stop wondering where your money went.

What Is Zero-Based Budgeting?

Zero-based budgeting means assigning every single dollar of your income a specific job—whether that's going toward bills, savings, or debt. By the end of your budgeting process, your income minus your expenses should equal zero.

It doesn't mean you have zero dollars—it means every dollar is accounted for.

Why It Works

Unlike traditional budgeting, where you might roll over last month's numbers or budget based on guesses, ZBB starts from scratch every month. You analyze what you need right now—not what you used to spend—and allocate accordingly.

This approach:

- Helps eliminate wasteful spending
- Forces you to prioritize needs over wants
- Creates a clear plan for your money
- Empowers you to take control of your financial future

For low-income households, where every dollar truly matters, ZBB is especially powerful. It gives structure, awareness, and purpose to your money.

Budgeting with Irregular or Low Income

If your income changes month to month, start by budgeting based on your lowest average monthly income.

When you earn more than expected, allocate the extra to savings or sinking funds (like car repairs, holidays, or back-to-school costs).

Pro tip: List essential expenses first. Cover your "four walls" (housing, utilities, food, transportation), then prioritize debt, savings, and finally—discretionary spending.

Breaking the Paycheck-to-Paycheck Cycle

When you're living paycheck to paycheck, it can feel like your money disappears as fast as it hits your account. ZBB stops that cycle by forcing you to plan how every dollar is used before the month begins.

This builds in intention—and over time, it gives you breathing room.

Even with limited income, knowing exactly where your money goes can help you stay on top of bills, build a small emergency fund, and slowly break the survival-mode loop.

Breaking out of the paycheck-to-paycheck cycle as a single mother on a low, fixed income can feel overwhelming, but there are several practical steps that can help you gain more financial stability.

Here's a mix of strategies that might help:

Track Your Spending

- Get clear on where your money is going by tracking all your expenses. It helps you identify areas where you might be able to cut back or find lower-cost alternatives.
- Use budgeting apps like Mint or YNAB (You Need A Budget) to stay organized.

Cut Back on Non-Essential Expenses

- Prioritize spending on essentials like rent, utilities, and groceries. See where you can eliminate or reduce discretionary spending (like subscriptions, dining out, or luxury items).

- Consider switching to more affordable services or brands for things like cell phone plans, insurance, or grocery shopping.

Increase Your Income

- Side Hustles: Find part-time or flexible gigs that you can do from home, such as freelancing, online tutoring, or delivering food. Websites like Upwork or Fiverr can be a good starting point.
- Ask for a Raise: If possible, negotiate a raise at your current job or look for better-paying opportunities. Even small raises can make a big difference over time.
- Sell Unused Items: Declutter your home and sell things you no longer need on platforms like Facebook Marketplace or eBay. This can bring in quick cash.

Build an Emergency Fund (Even Small Amounts)

- Start small: Even putting aside $10 or $20 a week can add up over time. Having an emergency fund will help prevent you from falling back into the cycle of debt when unexpected expenses arise.

Use Community Resources

- Many communities offer assistance programs that can help with food, utilities, and childcare. Check out your local food bank, WIC, or any state-sponsored programs for single mothers. This can free up money for savings or to pay down debt.
- Childcare assistance: Look for childcare subsidies or programs that may help reduce the cost of childcare so you can work more hours or take on side gigs.

Debt Management

- Consolidate or Refinance: If you have high-interest debt (like credit cards), consolidating or refinancing can lower your monthly payments. Research programs like debt consolidation loans or contact a non-profit credit counselor for help.
- Avoid New Debt: Try to avoid taking on new debt, especially high-interest loans or payday loans, as this can make your financial situation worse in the long run.

Focus on Long-Term Goals

- Skill Development: If possible, invest time in learning new skills (through free courses or online resources) to improve your job prospects and potentially earn a higher income in the future.
- Build Credit: If your credit score is low, working on improving it can help you qualify

for better financial products in the future, such as lower-interest loans.

Seek Out Financial Advice

- There are free or low-cost financial counseling services that can help you make a plan to get out of debt and increase your savings. Non-profits like National Foundation for Credit Counseling (NFCC) can help guide you through managing your finances.
- The road to financial freedom can be a gradual process, but taking small, consistent steps can help you build a better foundation for you and your children.

What do you feel might be the biggest hurdle for you right now in terms of getting started on these steps?

How to Build a Zero-Based Budget

Step 1: Determine Your Monthly Net Income

Calculate how much money you actually take home each month (after taxes). Include:

- Your paycheck(s)
- Side hustle income
- Child support, benefits, or other assistance

This is your total pool to work with.

Step 2: List All Monthly Expenses

Break them down into categories:

- Fixed (rent, insurance, car payments)
- Variable (groceries, gas, entertainment)
- Savings (emergency fund, sinking funds
- Debt repayment (credit cards, loans)

Step 3: Allocate Every Dollar

Now assign your income to your categories. By the end, your income minus your expenses = $0.

Example:

- Income: $2,500
- Rent: $1,000
- Groceries: $400
- Gas/transportation: $100

- Dining out: $100
- Entertainment: $50
- Debt repayment: $200
- Savings: $350

Total = $2,500

Every dollar has a job. No money is left floating.

Using Cash Envelopes with Zero-Based Budgeting

Now let's supercharge your ZBB with the cash envelope system. This hands-on method helps you stay on track by limiting spending to actual cash.

Step 4: Create Cash Envelopes for Variable Expenses

For categories like groceries, gas, and dining out:

- Withdraw cash and place it into labeled envelopes
- Only spend what's in the envelope

When it's gone, you're done spending in that category for the month

Example:

- Groceries envelope: $400
- Gas envelope: $100
- Dining out envelope: $100

No need for envelopes for fixed expenses like rent or digital subscriptions—they're already accounted for.

Step 5: Stick to the Plan

Throughout the month:

1. Spend only what's in each envelope
2. If you run out, don't borrow from other envelopes unless it's an emergency
3. Avoid using credit cards or dipping into savings unless it's a true necessity
   This builds discipline and makes you aware of how quickly money goes when there's no plan.

Step 6: Track Your Spending

Check your envelopes weekly. Notice if:

- You consistently run out in a certain category
- You have leftover funds
- You're overspending or underestimating a need

If your grocery envelope is empty by week three, maybe you need to increase it next month. If you always have cash left in "entertainment," you might reduce it and shift that money toward debt or savings.

Step 7: Review & Adjust Each Month

At the end of the month, reflect:

1. Did I stick to my budget?
2. Which envelopes worked? Which didn't?
3. Did I have leftover cash? Did I overspend?

Adjust your categories and amounts next month based on what you learned. ZBB is meant to evolve with you.

Step 8: Stay Consistent and Disciplined

Discipline is the secret weapon here. The cash envelope system works because it sets physical boundaries on spending.

Helpful tips:

- Try digital envelopes if carrying cash doesn't work for you (apps like Goodbudget or Qube Money)
- Start small. Use cash envelopes for just 1–2 categories at first
- Emergency fund first. Extra cash? Build that cushion
- Avoid credit cards. Only spend what you've planned

Why This System Works

Combining zero-based budgeting with the envelope system helps you:

- Take full control of your money
- Stop overspending
- Build savings
- Pay off debt
- Plan for emergencies

It creates structure and clarity—especially when money is tight. You don't need a higher income to feel secure.

You just need a plan.

Stick with it, track every month, and keep adjusting as life changes.

This is how you build habits, peace of mind, and eventually—financial freedom.

Zero-Based Budgeting 101

Reflection

1. How do I feel about assigning every dollar a job—does it bring me peace, anxiety, or resistance?
2. Have I been afraid to look too closely at where my money goes each month? Why?
3. What does financial discipline mean to me, and what has kept me from practicing it consistently?
4. How might building a budget that reflects my real life (not an ideal version) be an act of self-respect and healing?

Affirmation

I am the CEO of my finances.

Every dollar I manage is a declaration of my purpose and priorities.

I have the power to break the paycheck-to-paycheck cycle, one step at a time.

My income may be limited, but my wisdom and discipline are not.

Prayer

God, thank You for entrusting me with what I have—even when it feels like it's not enough.

Help me make wise, faith-filled decisions with each dollar.

Give me the courage to plan, the discipline to follow through, and the grace to begin again when I fall short.

Let budgeting be an act of worship—one that brings peace, provision, and progress. Amen.

Action

- Choose a day this week to build your first (or revised) zero-based budget.
- Write out your total income, all your expenses, and assign every dollar a job.
- Start with the essentials: shelter, food, transportation, and utilities.
- Create 1–2 cash envelopes for the categories you tend to overspend in (like food or personal care).
- Download a free budgeting worksheet or use a budgeting app to track everything.
- At the end of the month, review and reflect: What worked? What didn't? Adjust and try again.

Chapter 3: Cash Stuffing Basics

"Tell your money where to go, or you'll wonder where it went."

Now that you understand how zero-based budgeting (ZBB) works, it's time to take it one step further with a hands-on, visual method that makes budgeting real: Cash Stuffing.

Cash stuffing is more than just putting money into envelopes.

-It's a practical, visual, and empowering way to take back control of your finances—especially if you're trying to rein in spending or are overwhelmed by digital transactions.

What Is Cash Stuffing?

Cash stuffing is a budgeting method where you physically divide your cash into labeled envelopes (or folders, binders, or boxes), each representing a specific spending category. You only spend what's in the envelope for that category—and when the money is gone, you stop spending.

This method works best when paired with zero-based budgeting, since ZBB ensures every dollar is assigned a purpose and cash stuffing gives you a physical, easy-to-manage system for those categories you tend to overspend on.

46

The Psychology Behind Cash Stuffing

Why does this method work so well—especially for people who struggle with overspending?

Because you feel the money leaving your hands.

When you swipe a card, it's easy to detach from the transaction.

But when you count out actual bills and hand them over, it triggers awareness and accountability.

You can literally see your spending, and that makes a difference.

Cash stuffing works by:

1. Building discipline: You physically limit what you can spend.
2. Encouraging mindfulness: You pause and think before spending.
3. Creating visual progress: You see how much you have left.
4. Reducing impulse buying: You're less likely to make quick purchases with limited cash on hand.

How Cash Stuffing Complements Zero-Based Budgeting

Zero-based budgeting gives your money direction.

Cash stuffing makes sure you follow through.

When used together:

- ZBB allocates your income to specific categories.
- Cash stuffing controls how much you spend in each category.

Together, they prevent overspending, support saving, and keep your budget on track.

How to Start Cash Stuffing

Step 1: Choose Your Categories

Not all expenses need envelopes. Focus on variable or flexible spending where you tend to overspend. Some common categories include:

- Groceries
- Gas/transportation
- Dining out
- Entertainment
- Household items
- Personal care
- Miscellaneous/fun
- Kids/school supplies

Leave fixed expenses (rent, insurance, subscriptions) in your bank account and pay those electronically.

Step 2: Get Your Supplies

You don't need anything fancy. Start with:

- Basic envelopes (paper or plastic)
- A permanent marker to label each envelope
- A wallet, binder, or accordion folder to keep them organized

Optional:

- Budgeting printables or trackers
- A cash envelope binder with zipper pouches
- Decorative labels (if you want to make it fun!)

Step 3: Stuff Your Envelopes

After finalizing your zero-based budget for the month:

1. Withdraw the total amount of cash for all your stuffing categories.
2. Divide the money according to your budgeted amounts.
3. Place each amount into its labeled envelope.

Example:

- Groceries: $400

- Gas: $100
- Dining Out: $75
- Entertainment: $50
- Misc: $25

Total withdrawn: $650

Step 4: Spend from Envelopes Only

This is the golden rule: only spend what's in the envelope.

- If you're going grocery shopping, bring only your grocery envelope.

- If it's empty, you're done spending for that category.

- Don't "borrow" from other envelopes unless you revise your budget.

Step 5: Track Your Spending

You can track spending on:

- The back of each envelope
- A notebook or budget journal
- An app (if you prefer digital tracking with physical cash)

This helps you notice your habits and stay within your limits.

What If You Overspend or Underspend?

If you overspend:

- You'll need to either stop spending or reallocate from another envelope—but be intentional. Don't rob your savings or emergency fund unless absolutely necessary.

If you underspend:

Congrats! You can:

- Roll it over into next month's envelope
- Put it toward savings or an emergency fund
- Use it to pay extra on debt
  Every leftover dollar is an opportunity to move closer to your financial goals.

Digital Alternatives to Cash Stuffing

If carrying cash feels unsafe or impractical, try digital envelope budgeting:

- Apps like Goodbudget, Qube, or You Need a Budget (YNAB) simulate envelope budgeting on your phone.
- You can still assign categories and track spending without handling physical cash.
- Some banks now offer "bucket" features within savings accounts to simulate cash stuffing digitally.

Tips for Success

- Start with just a few categories. You don't need to stuff every expense. Begin with 2–3 problem areas.
- Stay organized. Keep your envelopes safe and labeled clearly.
- Make it a routine. Set a "stuffing day" every paycheck to stay consistent.
- Don't compare. Your system is for your goals. Whether it's $20 or $200, it's about intention—not amounts.
- Get the family involved. Use it as a teaching tool for kids or a way to share financial responsibilities with your partner.

The Power of Cash Stuffing

Cash stuffing might seem old-school, but its power lies in simplicity and visibility. It brings awareness, structure, and control into your everyday spending.

When used with zero-based budgeting, you're not just managing money—you're changing behavior. And that's the foundation of lasting financial freedom.

🐝 Reflection | Affirmation | Prayer | Action

Cash Stuffing Basics

Cash Stuffing Basics. This section continues the empowering, grace-filled tone while anchoring the practical budgeting method in deeper awareness and intention.

Reflection

1. How does handling cash physically make me feel—empowered, nervous, secure, or restricted?
2. What categories in my life tend to slip through the cracks financially?
3. Do I tend to overspend emotionally, impulsively, or out of habit?
4. How might setting boundaries with my money also help me set healthier boundaries in other areas of my life?

Affirmation

I am not afraid to look at my money.

I give every dollar direction and purpose.

Cash does not control me—I control it.

Even small amounts, handled with care, create big transformation.

Prayer

God, thank You for showing me that discipline is not punishment—it is protection.

Help me be intentional with what You've placed in my hands.

Give me clarity, consistency, and confidence as I build new habits.

Let this process not just organize my money but also calm my mind and reorder my priorities.

May even the smallest envelope reflect my trust in You. Amen.

Action

- Identify 2–3 categories where you tend to overspend. These are your starter envelopes.
- Choose a simple method—plain envelopes, a binder, or digital app—and set up your system.

- Withdraw only what you need in cash for those categories this pay period.
- Label, stuff, and commit: only spend from those envelopes.
- Track your spending. Notice where money flows easily and where it leaks. Adjust next month accordingly.
- If you underspend, celebrate the win! Redirect it to savings, debt, or next month's budget.

Chapter 4: Setting Up Your Financial Toolkit

"It's not just about discipline—it's about designing a system that fits your real life."

Budgeting isn't just about numbers—it's also about systems. And the truth is, no one system works for everyone.

Some people thrive with spreadsheets and digital apps. Others need physical binders and paper checklists.

If you're a mom, a caregiver, or managing chronic illness, you also need something that's accessible, low-maintenance, and realistic.

In this chapter, we'll build your personalized financial toolkit—one that meets you where you are and works with the time, energy, and focus you actually have.

Let's set you up for long-term success.

Why You Need a Toolkit

Think of your toolkit as the way you interact with your budget.

Budgeting is a plan.

Your toolkit is how you follow through on that plan.

A good financial toolkit should:

- Fit your lifestyle (digital or physical? quick or detailed?)
- Match your energy level (do you want to log in once a week or glance at a binder?)
- Make you feel calm and in control—not overwhelmed

You don't need 10 tools. Just the right ones that support your system.

Budget Binders, Envelopes, and Printables

Let's start with physical tools. If you're a tactile learner or need something visual, this section is for you.

Budget Binders

A budget binder is a great all-in-one place to track your goals, spending, bills, and progress. It can include:

- Monthly calendar
- Income + expense tracker
- Bill due dates
- Debt payoff tracker
- Savings goals
- Sinking funds log
- Cash stuffing envelopes (zippered pouches or slots)

What You'll Need:

- A 3-ring binder or discbound planner
- Printable budgeting sheets or inserts (many are free or affordable online)
- Dividers for categories (income, bills, savings, etc.)
- A pen or highlighters for color coding

Why it works:

It's visual. You see what's coming in and out, and it helps you stay consistent month after month.

Cash Envelopes

As discussed in Chapter 3, cash envelopes help you control spending by using actual cash in labeled envelopes. You can keep these in your binder, wallet, or a zip pouch system.

Pro tip: Make the system beautiful and personal.

Use washi tape, colors, stickers—whatever makes it fun for you. That personal touch helps create ownership and consistency.

Budget Printables

Printable budget worksheets give you structure without requiring digital tools.

You can print new ones every month or keep a master copy in your binder.

Examples:

- Monthly budget sheet
- Weekly check-in sheet
- No-spend tracker
- Savings thermometer
- Debt snowball tracker
- Expense log

Printables can be:

- Downloaded online
- Created in Canva or Google Docs
- Bought as part of a budgeting kit on Etsy

Budgeting Apps vs. Paper Systems

There's no "best" option—only what fits your lifestyle. Here's a quick breakdown to help you decide:

Budgeting Apps

Perfect for: people who are on-the-go, like automation, or prefer their phone.

Popular apps:

- EveryDollar – Simple, based on zero-based budgeting
- Goodbudget – Digital envelope system
- You Need a Budget (YNAB) – Powerful, but requires a learning curve
- Mint (free) or Rocket Money – Good for tracking, not as good for planning

Pros:

- Automatically tracks transactions (some apps sync with your bank)
- Can alert you to overspending
- Accessible from anywhere

Cons:

- May feel overwhelming or impersonal
- Sometimes too many features = distraction
- Might not work well if you use mostly cash

Paper Systems

Perfect for: visual learners, people trying to reduce screen time, or those who prefer slower, mindful budgeting.

Pros:

- Forces you to be intentional with every dollar
- Great for memory and learning through writing
- Can be personalized and creative

Cons:

- Manual tracking takes time
- Can be harder to adjust on-the-go

Hybrid Tip: Use an app to track income and fixed bills, and paper for your cash spending categories. Best of both worlds.

Accessibility Tips for Moms with Limited Energy or Mobility

Your budget system should serve you, not the other way around. Especially if you're juggling kids, managing fatigue, or living with chronic illness, you need tools that work even on low-energy days.

Here are real-life, compassionate tips for creating a sustainable system:

1. Keep It Visible

Out of sight = out of mind. Keep your binder, envelopes, or budget calendar somewhere easy to see—like your kitchen counter or nightstand.

2. Batch Budgeting

Do your budget all at once on a "high energy" day— once per paycheck or once a month. Break it into short 20-minute sessions if needed.

3. Use a Rolling To-Do List

Instead of trying to budget every day, keep a small notebook or sticky pad with 3–5 recurring financial check-ins:

- Check envelopes
- Pay bills
- Update budget sheet
- Adjust categories
- Count savings jars or goals

Do what you can, when you can. No shame in small steps.

4. Voice Notes & Reminders

Too tired to write things down? Use the voice recorder on your phone to remind yourself about your spending or ideas. Set recurring reminders for bill due dates or budget check-ins.

5. Color-Coding

Use colors to make your budget easier to process. Highlight fixed expenses in one color, flexible in another, savings goals in another. This creates an instant mental map, especially helpful on low-focus days.

6. Simplify, Simplify, Simplify

If it feels like too much, reduce your categories. Stick to 3–5 envelopes. Track only the biggest expenses. Pick one tracker to follow each month. Done is better than perfect.

Your Toolkit, Your Rules

You are the CEO of your household. You get to decide what tools, systems, and routines work best. Whether that's a binder, an app, a shoebox of receipts, or a voice memo budget check-in—it's all valid.

There is no "wrong" way to budget if it works for you. This toolkit is here to support you—not stress you out.

🐾 Reflection | Affirmation | Prayer | Action

Setting Up Your Financial Toolkit

Setting Up Your Financial Toolkit—designed with flexibility, grace, and real-life challenges in mind, especially for readers managing motherhood, limited energy, or chronic illness.

Reflection

1. What kind of budgeting system would truly fit my current lifestyle and capacity—not my ideal self, but my real self?
2. Have I been trying to force a method that doesn't work for me?
3. What tools make me feel calm and confident—and what tools just feel like clutter or pressure?
4. How can I give myself more permission to simplify, adapt, or rest in this area?

Affirmation

My system doesn't have to be perfect—it just has to work for me.

I am allowed to keep things simple, sustainable, and slow.

My peace matters more than someone else's productivity.

I choose tools that support me, not stress me out.

Prayer

Lord, thank You for being patient with me as I learn new ways to steward what You've given me.

Help me create a system that works with the life You've called me to—not one that burdens me, but one that blesses me.

Show me how to budget with grace, flexibility, and joy.

Teach me to embrace progress over perfection and to find peace in the process. Amen.

Action

- Pick one primary budgeting method: binder, app, printable, or hybrid. Don't overthink it— go with what feels doable.
- Set up a simple space for your tools (a kitchen drawer, binder pouch, or digital folder).
- Choose 2–3 printables, apps, or trackers you want to start with—keep it light.
- Make it visible: leave your toolkit somewhere you'll naturally see it.
- Schedule your next budget check-in on a high-energy day, even if it's just 15–20 minutes.
- Remind yourself: you can adjust any time. Your toolkit should grow with you.

Part II: Creating Your Budgeting System

Now that you have a toolkit in place, we'll talk about sinking funds—the secret to affording big expenses without breaking your monthly budget. You'll learn how to break down big costs (like holidays, school fees, or car repairs) into manageable monthly contributions, so nothing catches you off guard.

Chapter 5: Creating Your First Zero-Based Budget

"Budgeting isn't about restriction. It's about direction. You're the one steering the ship now."

Now that you've gathered your income and expenses, it's time to take the first real step: building your zero-based budget (ZBB).

In this chapter, we'll walk through the entire process step-by-step so you can confidently assign every dollar a job.

You'll learn how to put your essentials first, protect your health, and create a plan that reflects your values and reality—not someone else's.

Budget Every Dollar and Allocate Funds

At the heart of zero-based budgeting is this rule:

"Your income minus your expenses should equal zero".

That doesn't mean your bank account should be empty—it means every dollar is accounted for.

Whether it's paying rent, buying groceries, saving for a doctor's visit, or setting aside money for birthdays, each dollar has a name and a purpose.

Here's the process:

1. Start with your total monthly income (after taxes).
2. List all of your expenses—essentials, debt payments, savings goals, and even fun money.
3. Allocate money to each category until every dollar has a job.

The goal: your income – expenses = $0. That's a zero-based budget.

No loose change hanging out in your checking account (besides maybe a small buffer of $50–$100 for bank fluctuations).

The rest? It gets to work.

Remember: You are the boss. You tell your money what to do—not the other way around.

Step-by-Step Walkthrough

1. Calculate Monthly Income

Tally all sources of income (job, side hustles, benefits, etc.).

Use your net income (after taxes).

2. List Expenses by Category
Break them down into:
- Essentials (housing, food, utilities, transportation)
- Health needs (medications, appointments)
- Debt repayment
- Savings & emergency fund
- Discretionary (entertainment, dining out, hobbies)

3. Assign Every Dollar
- Allocate based on your priorities.
- Start with essentials, then assign to savings and debt.
- What's left goes to wants.
- Check the Math
- Total income minus expenses = $0

If there's money left: allocate it.

If you're over budget: adjust down in non-essentials.

Prioritize Essentials & Maintain Discipline

Stick to your needs first—especially when income is limited.

Try using the 50/30/20 rule as a starting point:

- 50% to needs (rent, food, transportation)
- 30% to wants (non-essentials, fun)
- 20% to savings and debt

This isn't a rule—it's a guide. Adjust it to fit your life. For example, if you have high medical costs or are focused on paying off debt, you might go 60/20/20 or 70/10/20.

Discipline and consistency are what turn a budget into results. Follow your budget each month, track your spending weekly, and review your categories often.

Making Room for Self-Care and Emergencies

Your budget should also reflect your reality. That includes:

- Medical needs
- Therapy or mental health support
- Restorative activities
- Buffer money for low-energy weeks

Include a line for self-care, even if it's $20/month. A small budget for peace of mind can prevent burnout and breakdown.

Also, start building an emergency fund—even if it's just $10/month. Life happens. A flat tire, a sick day, a missed paycheck. Having money set aside for surprises gives you power and peace.

Review & Adjust Regularly

This isn't a one-and-done process. Your life will change—and your budget should too.

Every month:

- Review what worked
- Look at what categories went over
- Reassign money based on actual spending

Over time, your budget becomes a reflection of what you truly value—not what you used to think was important.

Avoid Lifestyle Creep

One of the biggest budgeting pitfalls? As your income increases, your spending increases just as fast. This is called lifestyle creep.

Instead of upgrading every category:

- Keep your living expenses stable
- Increase your savings rate
- Pay off debt faster

Remember: It's a marathon, not a sprint. Progress is progress.

🦋 Reflection | Affirmation | Prayer | Action

Creating Your First Zero-Based Budget

Reflection

1. Are you currently telling your money where to go—or just watching it disappear?

Think about how you've handled money in the past. Were you reactive, trying to fix things after the fact? Or did you have a plan and a purpose for every dollar?

This chapter reminds us that budgeting is not punishment—it's protection. It's about being intentional with the resources you've been given. Even if it's not much right now, it's still yours to steward wisely.

2. What areas of your budget reflect your values? What areas feel out of alignment with who you want to be?

"Whoever can be trusted with very little can also be trusted with much..." —Luke 16:10 NIV

Affirmation

I am not powerless with my money.

Every dollar I earn has purpose, and I am equipped to create a plan that reflects my real life, my priorities, and my values.

God gives me wisdom to manage what I have well, and I choose to walk in financial stewardship—not fear.

Prayer

Lord, thank You for the provision You've placed in my hands—whether it feels like a little or a lot.

Help me to honor You with how I use it.

Give me clarity as I create a budget that supports my health, my family, and my calling.

Where there's been chaos, bring peace. Where there's been avoidance, give me the courage to take small, steady steps.

Teach me to assign every dollar with wisdom, not worry, and help me trust that You will continue to meet every need—one faithful step at a time. Amen.

Action

Create your first zero-based budget.

- Start with your net monthly income.
- List your expenses by category: essentials, health, debt, savings, and wants.
- Allocate every dollar until income minus expenses equals zero.
- Include a small amount for self-care and emergency savings—even $10 counts.
- Review and adjust after two weeks: What worked? What needs tweaking?

Bonus Tip: Name your budget.

Give it a title that inspires you—like "Healing & Hope Plan" or "Freedom Tracker."

Make it feel personal and powerful.

Chapter 6: Creating a Sinking Fund System

"If you know it's coming, you can plan for it. That's what sinking funds are all about."

Unexpected expenses are often not unexpected at all. Birthdays, back-to-school season, holiday gifts, car repairs—they come every year. So why do they always feel like emergencies?

The answer: sinking funds.

What Is a Sinking Fund?

A sinking fund is money you set aside each month for a future expense.

Instead of panicking when a big bill hits, you've been preparing for it all along—in small, manageable amounts.

You can create a sinking fund for:

- Birthdays
- Holidays
- Back-to-school costs
- Medical bills
- Annual car registration
- Travel
- Home or car repairs
- Kids' sports or extracurriculars

How to Start a Sinking Fund

List predictable, irregular expenses

Think through the year ahead.

What do you always forget to plan for?

1. **Estimate the total cost**
   For example:

Christmas gifts = $600

School supplies = $150

Car maintenance = $400

2. **Divide by the number of months until due**

$600 ÷ 12 months = $50/month

$150 ÷ 6 months = $25/month

3. **Create a savings envelope or tracker for each fund**

You can use physical cash envelopes or digital sub-savings accounts.

4. **Add to your sinking funds each month in your ZBB (zero base budget)**

These amounts are now part of your monthly budget. They're just as important as rent or groceries.

Benefits of Sinking Funds

- Eliminates surprise bills
- Reduces stress around "special" times of year
- Prevents debt from creeping back in
- Builds financial confidence and discipline

Tips for Managing Sinking Funds

1. Start small – Focus on 2–3 important categories first.
2. Automate it – Use automatic transfers to savings accounts if possible.
3. Track progress visually – Color in a printable or use a savings thermometer.
4. Roll over unused money – If you don't spend it all, leave it for next year or reassign it.

A Note on Priorities

If you're still working on building an emergency fund or paying off debt, start with one or two high-impact sinking funds. Choose ones that will give you relief—like holiday gifts or car repairs.

Once you have a rhythm, expand.

Moving Forward

Sinking funds are your secret weapon for building financial stability. They turn big, scary bills into tiny, manageable pieces.

🐾 Reflection | Affirmation | Prayer | Action

Creating a Sinking Fund System

—designed to help shift from reacting to preparing, even when funds are tight.

"If you know it's coming, you can plan for it."

Reflection

Have you ever called something an emergency, when deep down, you knew it was coming?

Sinking funds are a grace-filled way to prepare without panic.

They invite you to honor what matters in your life—birthdays, rest, car repairs, your kids' needs—and give yourself room to breathe financially.

Ask yourself:

1. What expenses always sneak up on me?
2. Which events do I want to plan for with peace, not pressure?
3. What would it feel like to have margin—not just money—in place?

   "The plans of the diligent lead surely to abundance..." —Proverbs 21:5 ESV

Affirmation

I plan ahead not out of fear, but out of faith and wisdom.

God equips me to prepare for what matters most.

Small steps today create freedom tomorrow.

I am no longer caught off guard—I am walking in readiness and peace.

Prayer

Lord, thank You for teaching me how to prepare with wisdom and faith.

Show me what to set aside today so I can step into tomorrow with confidence.

Help me prioritize what matters, and to trust that You'll stretch what I have as I steward it well.

Even when the numbers feel small, remind me that I'm sowing seeds that lead to peace and provision. Amen.

Action

- Choose 2–3 sinking fund categories that bring the most stress or surprise—start there.
- Estimate the total cost and divide it by the number of months until the expense is due.
- Add those amounts to your zero-based budget this month.
- Set up a savings tracker (printable, app, or envelope).
- Celebrate every contribution—even $5 counts. You're building peace in pieces.

Grace Note:

You don't need to be rich to prepare—you just need to be consistent.

Start small.

Stay faithful.

Watch the peace grow.

Chapter 7: Cash Envelope Categories That Work

"Budgeting works best when it reflects your real life—not someone else's."

One-size-fits-all doesn't apply when it comes to managing money, especially if you live with unique challenges like health conditions, limited energy, or caregiving responsibilities.

That's why your cash envelope categories should be tailored to your needs.

In this chapter, you'll learn how to break down fixed and variable expenses, create envelopes for irregular costs, and build a flexible system that works whether you're using physical cash, digital tools, or both.

Fixed Expenses vs. Variable Expenses

Before you set up your envelopes, divide your expenses into two main categories:

- Fixed Expenses – These stay the same each month (rent, insurance, subscriptions).
- Variable Expenses – These fluctuate (groceries, gas, personal spending, medical supplies).

You don't need envelopes for every fixed expense—just pay those through your bank or card as usual. Focus your envelope system on variable expenses you can control.

How to Plan for Irregular or Annual Expenses

Not every expense shows up monthly.

Think holidays, insurance premiums, school clothes, or car maintenance.

These "irregular" costs can blow up your budget if you're not prepared.

Solution: Sinking Funds

- Set up a separate savings account or envelope for each irregular expense.

- Estimate the total amount needed and divide by the number of months until it's due.

- Contribute a small amount each month.

When the bill arrives, the money is already there.

No scrambling, no debt, no stress.

ꙮ Reflection | Affirmation | Prayer | Action

Cash Envelope Categories That Work for You

"Budgeting works best when it reflects your real life—not someone else's."

Reflection

Budgeting isn't about perfection or imitation—it's about intentionality and freedom. When you tailor your cash envelope categories to your own life, you create space for peace, not pressure.

Consider:

1. What categories in your life are often neglected or overspent?
2. Are you trying to fit your budget into someone else's mold instead of creating your own?
3. Where can you add more grace—like a buffer, a "fun" fund, or medical supplies—to reflect your real needs?

"Let all things be done decently and in order." — 1 Corinthians 14:40 (KJV)

Affirmation

My budget honors my reality—not someone else's ideal.

I am allowed to create financial systems that reflect my values, health, and family.

I give myself permission to be flexible and to grow.

There is wisdom in building a budget that breathes.

Prayer

God, thank You for being present in every detail of my life—including my finances.

Help me build a system that reflects not just what I owe, but what I need.

Give me courage to choose categories that make sense for my season, and wisdom to adjust them without guilt.

Remind me that my worth isn't found in balance sheets but in Your grace. Amen.

Action

- Review your current envelope categories—are they working for you or stressing you out?
- Add one new category that reflects a current need or priority (e.g., health, rest, therapy, joy).
- Remove or revise a category that no longer serves your goals.
- Create a "buffer" or "fun" fund—even if it's small—to build flexibility and joy into your plan.
- Explore whether physical cash, prepaid cards, or digital apps suit your lifestyle best. Adjust boldly.

Gentle Reminder: Your envelope system is yours. Make it fit your life. Keep what works. Leave what doesn't.

God's provision meets you right where you are.

Chapter 8: Creating a Buffer Fund

Life happens.

Maybe groceries cost a little more this week, or gas prices jumped. That's why it's smart to set aside a small buffer—$20, $50, or $100—as part of your monthly budget.

Keep this in a separate envelope or digital category, and only use it when absolutely necessary.

A buffer fund adds flexibility without throwing off your whole system.

Using a Mix of Cash and Digital Envelopes

You don't have to use physical cash for everything. Some expenses—like online purchases, subscriptions, or bills—are best managed digitally.

Use budgeting apps like:

- Goodbudget
- EveryDollar
- YNAB (You Need A Budget)

These apps simulate envelopes digitally, allowing you to stay organized while paying online or with a debit card.

Roll Over or Reallocate Extra Cash

At the end of the month, if you have money left in an envelope, you've got options:

- Roll It Over: Let it accumulate for next month (great for categories like gas or groceries).
- Reallocate: Move it to savings, an emergency fund, or debt repayment.

Either option brings you closer to your goals. Don't let leftover money sit aimlessly—put it to work.

Track Your Net Worth

Zero-based budgeting focuses on day-to-day spending. But if you want to see the big picture, track your net worth:

- Assets (what you own) – Liabilities (what you owe) = Net Worth

Tracking this monthly or quarterly helps you monitor long-term progress, not just monthly survival.

Emergency Fund Comes First

Before tackling debt aggressively or saving for big goals, build a basic emergency fund—even $500 can prevent financial disaster.

Emergency funds protect you from dipping into envelopes or using credit when the unexpected happens. This is your financial safety net. Prioritize it.

Cash Not Your Thing? Try Prepaid Debit Cards

If carrying cash feels unsafe or inconvenient, try loading specific categories (like groceries or gas) onto prepaid debit cards or separate bank accounts. You still spend within limits—it just looks different.

This is especially helpful for digital-first people or those managing money on the go.

Review and Adjust Your Budget Often

Check in with your budget at least once a quarter—more if your income or expenses change.

Ask yourself:

1. Did any categories go consistently over or under?
2. Have your priorities shifted?
3. Are you meeting your goals?

Your system should grow with you. Make changes confidently—this is your budget, not a rulebook.

Include a Reward or "Fun" Fund

Yes, you're budgeting—but don't forget to live. Set aside a small amount each month for treats or fun activities.

Whether it's coffee, a craft supply, or a night out, a "joy fund" helps prevent burnout and resentment. A little planned pleasure goes a long way in helping you stick with the system long-term.

Automate Your Savings

Make saving easy by automating transfers into your emergency fund, sinking funds, or long-term savings. When the money moves before you see it, you're less tempted to spend it.

Paying yourself first builds habits, not just balances.

Summary: Fine-Tuning Your System

Your budget is a living tool—not a straightjacket. Here are some final tips to optimize your envelope system:

- Plan for irregular/annual expenses with sinking funds
- Include a buffer for flexibility
- Use digital envelopes when cash isn't ideal
- Roll over or reallocate leftover cash
- Track your net worth for long-term vision
- Prioritize building an emergency fund early
- Adjust as your income, goals, or life changes
- Don't forget a reward or fun fund—it's essential

With zero-based budgeting and your customized envelope system, you're not just surviving—you're taking control.

Stick with it, and you'll build a financial life that reflects your values, supports your needs, and brings you real peace of mind.

Chapter 9: Consistency Without Burnout

"Discipline makes the difference—but grace makes it sustainable."

Sticking to a budget takes effort, especially when you're juggling real-life challenges like health issues, fatigue, caregiving, or financial anxiety.

This chapter is about building a routine you can actually maintain—without burnout, shame, or perfectionism.

Budgeting isn't about being flawless. It's about being consistent, intentional, and kind to yourself in the process.

Building a Budgeting Routine

A strong financial routine doesn't have to be complicated—it just needs to be consistent.

Start with the basics:

1. Create your zero-based budget at the beginning of each month.
2. Track your spending weekly or biweekly using a method that works for your energy and lifestyle.
3. Review and reflect monthly to adjust based on what worked—and what didn't.

Tools to track your budget:

- Digital: Apps like EveryDollar, YNAB, or Goodbudget
- Analog: Spreadsheets (Google Sheets, Excel) or a notebook
- Hybrid: Use digital for fixed expenses, cash envelopes for variable ones

Example Zero-Based Budget

Monthly Income: $3,000

Fixed Expenses

- Rent: $1,000
- Utilities: $150
- Insurance (health, car): $200
- Subscriptions (Netflix, gym): $50

Total Fixed: $1,400

Variable Expenses

- Groceries: $300
- Transportation/Gas: $100
- Dining Out: $100

Total Variable: $500

Savings

- Emergency Fund: $300
- Retirement: $200

Total Savings: $500

Debt Repayment

- Credit Card: $100
- Student Loans: $100

Total Debt: $200

Grand Total: $3,000

Leftover: $0 – Every dollar has a job.

Zero-based budgeting works because it gives your money direction.

It helps you:

1. Track your income and expenses
2. Justify your spending choices
3. Adjust when needed
4. Make intentional financial decisions

The more you practice, the more confident you'll become.

Monthly Reviews and Adjustments

Budgeting isn't "set it and forget it." Life shifts, so your budget should too.

At the end of each month:

- Review your spending: Where did you go over? Where did you underspend?
- Check for unexpected costs: Emergencies, events, forgotten bills
- Compare actual vs. budgeted amounts
- Adjust your plan for next month accordingly

Ask yourself:

1. Did I meet my savings goals?
2. Did I have enough in my envelopes?
3. Did any categories surprise me?
4. Is there anything I can do differently next month?

Examples of adjustments:

- Overspent on groceries? Consider increasing that category next month and cutting back dining out.
- Underspent on gas? Reallocate to savings or your emergency fund.
- Got a raise? Increase your savings or debt payments first before adjusting lifestyle spending.

Each month is a new opportunity to fine-tune your system. It's not failure—it's feedback.

Resting Without Quitting: Grace Over Guilt

Budgeting can feel overwhelming, especially when energy or focus is limited. That's why grace must be part of your financial plan.

You will have off days. You'll forget to track receipts. You might overspend. That's okay.

Here's how to rest without quitting:

- Set realistic targets. Don't budget for a fantasy version of your life. Budget for the real you.
- Build in buffer space. Life isn't perfect—leave margin for the unexpected.
- Celebrate small wins. Made all your cash envelope withdrawals on time? That counts.
- Don't shame yourself. Learn from a slip-up and move on. Tomorrow is a new budget day.

You're doing this for the long haul. Aim for progress, not perfection.

How to Adjust Without Overwhelm

If your budget feels tight, off, or just not working:

Try this checklist:

- Reevaluate fixed expenses. Can you renegotiate bills or pause subscriptions?

- Adjust savings or debt goals if your income changed.
- Cut back on non-essentials if spending is tight.
- Revisit your priorities: Are you budgeting for what matters most right now?

Remember: Flexibility keeps your budget sustainable. Rigidity leads to burnout.

Consistency Is a Practice, Not a Personality Trait

You don't need to be naturally organized or financially savvy to be consistent. You just need a system that works with you, not against you.

Set a simple routine:

- Pick one day each week to check your budget (e.g., Sundays)
- Keep a "budget check-in" journal or checklist
- Use reminders or alarms to stay on track
- Keep your tools (binders, envelopes, cards) easy to access

The more automated and routine it becomes, the less mental energy it takes.

Key Takeaways: Sustainable Budgeting

- Build a realistic routine using tools that fit your life

- Track weekly, review monthly, and adjust regularly
- Give yourself grace when things don't go as planned

- Stay flexible—your budget should evolve as you do
- Celebrate your effort, not just your results

Budgeting isn't just about numbers—it's about habits, health, and hope. You're creating something that supports your life—not another source of stress.

So breathe. Tweak what needs tweaking. Rest when you need to. And most importantly—keep going.

✌ Reflection | Affirmation | Prayer | Action
Consistency Without Burnout

Reflection

Budgeting can feel like a constant uphill battle, especially when you're already managing chronic illness, caregiving, or financial anxiety.

But what if the goal wasn't perfection, but peace? What if discipline and grace could work together?

Take a moment to reflect:

1. What part of budgeting feels most draining for you?
2. Where can you add grace—not guilt—into your financial routine?
3. What would consistency look like if it was rooted in compassion, not criticism?

Affirmation

"I build financial consistency with grace, not pressure. I am free to grow at my own pace. My small steps matter."

Prayer

God, Thank You for reminding me that consistency doesn't mean perfection.

Help me create a routine that honors both my financial goals and my physical limitations.

When I feel tired or behind, remind me that rest is not failure.

Give me the wisdom to adjust without shame, and the courage to keep showing up.

Teach me to be faithful with what I have and gracious with myself when I fall short. Amen.

Action

Choose one of the following this week:

- Designate a weekly "budget check-in" day—even 15 minutes counts.
- Create a "Grace Note" in your journal: a place where you celebrate small wins and lessons learned.
- Review last month's budget without judgment—just observe and adjust.

If you've been holding your breath financially, this is your reminder: you can exhale.

Part III: Managing Life's Expenses

Discover how physical or digital cash envelopes and sinking funds can reduce stress and improve spending discipline. You'll learn to plan for regular bills, medical costs, and surprise expenses without panic.

Chapter 10: Managing Medical Expenses on a Budget

"Your health matters. So does your financial peace. This chapter helps you protect both."

Medical costs can be overwhelming. From doctor visits and prescriptions to insurance premiums and surprise ER bills, healthcare expenses have the power to throw your entire budget off track. But you don't have to let them.

This chapter is your guide to managing medical costs with clarity and control.

You'll learn how to track bills, prepare for the unexpected, and find help when you need it—without letting health expenses derail your goals.

Tracking Bills and Insurance

The first step to managing medical costs is getting organized.

Create a Medical Expense Log

Whether you use a spreadsheet, a printable tracker, or a notebook, start keeping track of:

- Appointments and services received
- Dates of service
- Provider names
- Charges billed
- Insurance payments

- Your responsibility (copay, coinsurance, deductible)
- Payment due dates and receipts

This log will help you spot errors, track what's been paid, and stay on top of deadlines to avoid late fees or collections.

Understand Your Insurance Plan

Take time to review:

- Your deductible (the amount you pay before insurance kicks in)
- Copay/coinsurance (your share of the cost after deductible)
- Out-of-pocket max (the most you'll pay in a year before insurance covers 100%)
- What's covered vs. not covered

Knowing these terms helps you budget realistically and prevents surprise bills.

Set Up a Folder or Binder System

Keep all medical paperwork in one place:

- Insurance EOBs (Explanation of Benefits)
- Bills from providers
- Payment receipts
- Appeal letters (if needed)

Use labeled folders or dividers: Insurance, Bills, Prescriptions, Receipts, Correspondence.

Finding Resources and Assistance Programs

If you're struggling to pay medical bills or access care, you are not alone. There are programs and strategies that can help.

Hospital Financial Assistance Programs

Many nonprofit hospitals offer charity care or sliding scale assistance based on income. Even if you've already received care, you can apply after the fact.

Ask about:

- Income-based payment plans
- Debt forgiveness programs
- Financial aid forms

Pro tip: Call the billing office directly and ask for their financial assistance policy.

Prescription Assistance

If prescriptions are breaking your budget, consider:

- GoodRx or RxSaver: Compare pharmacy prices and use free coupons
- Manufacturer copay cards: Some drug makers offer discounts

- Patient Assistance Programs (PAPs): Free meds for qualifying patients (e.g., through NeedyMeds.org or RxAssist.org)
- $4 prescription programs: At Walmart, Kroger, and other chains

Community Health Resources

Check with:

- Community clinics or Federally Qualified Health Centers (FQHCs)
- Local health departments
- Nonprofits offering help with chronic illnesses or disabilities
- State or county medical aid programs

Search your ZIP code on 211.org or call 2-1-1 to find free or low-cost local services.

Planning for Unexpected Health Costs

Unexpected illness, accidents, or flare-ups can be financially devastating.

But you can cushion the blow with some smart planning.

Build a Medical Sinking Fund

Treat healthcare like any other irregular expense (like car maintenance or holidays). Set up a sinking fund envelope or savings account and contribute monthly, even if it's just $10–$50.

Over time, this stash becomes your buffer for:

- Copays
- Prescriptions
- Supplies (like glasses, mobility aids, or OTC meds)
- ER visits or urgent care

Budget for Ongoing Needs

If you or a family member has a chronic condition, factor recurring costs into your monthly zero-based budget:

- Regular prescriptions
- Medical supplies (test strips, braces, etc.)
- Therapy or rehab
- Home health care
- Being proactive reduces stress—and surprises.
- Consider Supplemental Insurance
- If your health situation is complex, look into:
- Medicaid (if you qualify)
- Medicare Advantage or Medigap plans (for Medicare users)

Short-term disability or critical illness insurance (if available through your employer)

These can help reduce out-of-pocket burdens in the long term.

Tips for Managing Medical Debt

If you already have unpaid medical bills:

Don't ignore them. Call the provider and ask about:

- Interest-free payment plans
- Settlement offers (some bills can be reduced if paid in full)
- Pausing collections while applying for financial aid
- Dispute errors. Medical billing errors are common. Review EOBs carefully and request itemized bills.
- Avoid using credit cards. Instead, try to work out a direct payment plan with no interest.

Know your rights. Medical debt now has more protections on your credit report.

Bills under $500 and those in collections (less than 1 year old) may no longer impact your score.

Takeaways: Staying Healthy and Financially Grounded

Medical expenses are real—and they can be overwhelming. But with a plan, support, and a little structure, you can manage them without losing peace of mind.

Your Medical Expense Toolkit:

1. Track every bill and insurance statement
2. Understand your plan and know what's covered
3. Use folders or binders to stay organized
4. Seek out prescription and care assistance
5. Create a sinking fund for recurring or surprise health costs
6. Ask for help—financial aid exists for a reason
7. Protect your credit and negotiate debt with confidence

You're not failing if medical bills feel hard to manage—you're navigating a tough system. And you're doing your best.

With the right tools and support, you can protect your health and your budget.

🐝 Reflection | Affirmation | Prayer | Action

Managing Medical Expenses on a Budget

"Your health matters. So does your financial peace."

Reflection

1. Have I been avoiding or feeling anxious about medical bills or insurance paperwork?
2. Where in my health journey do I feel financially vulnerable—or unsupported?
3. What systems (if any) do I currently have in place to track or plan for healthcare expenses?
4. How might clarity in this area give me back peace and power?

Affirmation

I can care for my health and my finances with wisdom and grace.

I am not powerless—God gives me strategy, support, and strength for every need.

Even when bills pile up, I will not panic. I will take one step at a time.

I deserve healing without shame and financial peace without fear.

Prayer

Dear Lord,

You are my Provider and my Healer.

Thank You for sustaining me through every appointment, diagnosis, and decision.

Help me steward my medical needs with courage, clarity, and calm.

Give me discernment as I navigate insurance, billing, and assistance programs.

Send the right resources, advocates, and answers at the right time.

When I feel overwhelmed, anchor me in peace.

When I feel alone, remind me You are near—and so are the people who care.

Help me remember: I don't have to figure it all out in one day.

Give me grace to ask for help, strength to take action, and wisdom to rest when needed. Amen.

Action

1. Create or update your medical expense log with bills, dates, and notes.
2. Make one call to an insurance rep, doctor's office, or billing department this week to clarify or negotiate a bill.
3. Download and print a medical folder checklist or organize paperwork into labeled folders (e.g., Bills, Prescriptions, EOBs).
4. Research local prescription discount programs or hospital financial aid—and apply if needed.
5. Start a sinking fund for future health costs, even if it's just $5–$10 to begin.

Remember: Protecting your peace is part of protecting your health.

Chapter 11: Raising Kids on a Budget

"It's not about how much you spend—it's about the love, structure, and creativity you give your children."

Raising kids is a beautiful, exhausting, and expensive journey. Between diapers, meals, clothes, school supplies, and birthday parties, the costs can feel like they never stop.

But the truth is—you can raise happy, well-rounded children without breaking your budget.

In this chapter, we'll cover how to prioritize what truly matters, teach your kids about money from a young age, feed your family affordably, and still find ways to make life joyful.

Teaching Children About Money

It's never too early to start teaching kids about finances. When you involve your children in budgeting and spending conversations, you're not just surviving on a budget—you're breaking generational cycles.

Make Money Visible and Real

For young kids, money can feel abstract—especially in a world of digital payments. Use visuals:

- Let them help count cash during envelope stuffing.
- Use clear jars for saving, spending, and giving.
- Talk through simple decisions: "We're choosing this cereal because it's on sale."

Age-Appropriate Lessons

Ages 3–6:

- Start with basics like coins, needs vs. wants, and waiting to buy something.
- Read books like "A Chair for My Mother" or "Bunny Money" to introduce money ideas.

Ages 7–12:

- Give a small allowance and help them divide it into save/spend/give jars.
- Let them budget for a small shopping trip or help meal plan within a set grocery amount.

Teens:

- Include them in household budgeting or show them how bills work.
- Help them open a teen checking account or savings account.
- Teach about credit, debt, and student loans before college.

Use Real-Life Teaching Moments

Involve your kids in:

- Grocery shopping and comparing prices.
- Saving for big purchases like school clothes or a class trip.
- Donating to causes they care about.

Every experience is a chance to raise a financially wise adult.

Budget-Friendly Meals and Routines

Feeding a family on a tight budget can feel like a full-time job. But with some planning and strategy, you can stretch your grocery dollars while still nourishing your family.

Smart Grocery Planning

- Meal plan weekly: Choose meals based on what's on sale and what you already have.
- Shop with a list—and stick to it.
- Buy in bulk when it makes sense (especially for staples like rice, beans, oats, frozen veggies).
- Use generic/store brands instead of name brands.

Cheap and Healthy Meal Ideas

- Breakfast: Overnight oats, eggs and toast, homemade muffins, smoothies
- Lunch: Quesadillas, rice bowls, pasta salad, PB&J with fruit
- Dinner: Sheet pan meals, soups, casseroles, slow cooker stews

Batch cooking and freezing extras can also save time and money.

Use SNAP, WIC, and Local Food Resources if Needed

If you qualify, these programs can provide essential support. Check:

- SNAP (Supplemental Nutrition Assistance Program)
- WIC (Women, Infants, and Children)
- Local food banks or school food programs

These are here for families like yours. There's no shame in using them—your kids deserve to be nourished.

Frugal Family Fun

Joy doesn't have to come with a price tag. Children remember how they felt, not how much you spent.

Low-Cost Activities

- Library visits and free local events

- DIY movie night with popcorn and homemade tickets
- Backyard camping or indoor picnics
- Nature walks and scavenger hunts
- Cooking or crafting together with what you have at home

Many communities offer free museum days, splash pads, family fitness events, or community fairs—look them up monthly and plan around them.

Birthdays and Holidays on a Budget

You don't need to go into debt to make memories:

- Host small gatherings at home or the park.
- Do potluck-style food with family and friends.
- Get creative with homemade decorations or baked goods.
- Give experience gifts: a coupon for one-on-one time, a special outing, or a day of "yes."

What matters is making your child feel loved and seen—not how much you spend.

Parenting with Stability, Not Perfection

Your kids don't need perfection. They need stability. Even when money is tight, budgeting allows you to provide:

- A safe home

- Consistent meals
- Emotional presence
- Predictable routines
- Open, honest conversations about life—including finances

The greatest gift you can give your children is not material—it's your attention, your values, and your love. A solid budget helps protect that.

Takeaways: Raising Kids with Financial Intention

Raising kids on a budget requires flexibility, creativity, and heart. But it's absolutely possible—and it builds a powerful foundation for their future.

Parenting on a Budget: Your Essentials

- Involve your kids in age-appropriate money talks
- Teach saving, spending, and giving early
- Plan and shop smart for meals
- Use assistance programs without guilt when needed
- Prioritize free or low-cost joy
- Stay focused on stability over perfection

Remember: what your child needs most is you. Not the latest toy. Not a perfect home. Just your steady, loving presence and the security of knowing you're doing your best. And you are.

✤ Reflection | Affirmation | Prayer | Action

Raising Kids on a Budget

"It's not about how much you spend—it's about the love, structure, and creativity you give your children."

Reflection

Raising children on a limited budget may feel like a daily balancing act—stretching dollars while trying to create a safe, joyful, and nurturing home.

But it's not about how much you can buy; it's about the presence you give, the lessons you teach, and the love you show.

Ask yourself:

1. Am I placing more pressure on myself to provide stuff than to provide stability?
2. What are some ways my children already feel secure and loved—regardless of money?
3. How can I invite my kids into our budgeting journey without placing fear on their shoulders?

Affirmation

My children are blessed not because of what I buy, but because of how I love.

I am building a legacy of wisdom, contentment, and joy.

I parent with creativity, strength, and intention— even on a budget.

Prayer

God, thank You for entrusting me with these little lives.

On days when my wallet feels empty, fill my heart with peace. Teach me to lead with love, not lack.

Help me model generosity, gratitude, and wisdom. Provide for our needs and show me how to multiply what we have through Your grace.

Remind me that I don't have to be perfect to be the parent my child needs—I just have to be present. Amen.

Action

- Choose one age-appropriate money activity to do with your child this week (e.g., coin sorting, budgeting a snack trip, opening a savings jar).
- Write out a simple weekly meal plan using foods you already have or that are on sale.
- Look up one free local activity or event for the week and add it to your calendar.
- Identify one area where you can simplify or save (e.g., reusable school supplies, library books instead of new ones, batch cooking).
- Speak one encouraging sentence over your child today about who they are—not what they have.

Chapter 12: Debt Payoff Strategies

Debt can feel like a heavy weight, especially when it's tied to hardship, unexpected expenses, or cycles of survival spending.

But debt doesn't define your future—it's a challenge, not a sentence. The key is finding a plan that matches your mindset, your financial reality, and your long-term goals.

In this chapter, we'll explore the most effective ways to tackle debt, maintain stability while doing it, and understand when alternative paths may be the best option.

Snowball vs. Avalanche: Two Proven Methods

When you're staring at a pile of bills, it's easy to feel overwhelmed. That's where debt repayment strategies like the Snowball and Avalanche methods come in.

The **Snowball Method** involves paying off your smallest debts first while making minimum payments on the others. As each small debt disappears, you gain momentum and motivation— like a snowball rolling downhill and gaining size.

Best for: People who need quick wins and emotional encouragement to stick with the process.

The **Avalanche Method** focuses on interest rates. You pay off the debt with the highest interest rate first, while making minimum payments on the rest. This saves the most money over time.
Best for: Those focused on math and minimizing long-term costs.

Which is better? There's no one right answer—it depends on your personality. If motivation is hard to maintain, snowball might help. If high interest is dragging you down, avalanche can be more efficient.

Budgeting While Paying Off Medical Debt

Medical debt can be especially demoralizing. It's often unexpected, large, and not tied to anything you "bought." But it still must be managed with care.

Here are some ways to balance medical debt with daily life:

- Prioritize essentials first. Food, housing, and basic utilities come before debt payments. Always.
- Negotiate medical bills. Call providers to ask for itemized bills and review them for errors. Many are negotiable.

- Look for payment plans or financial aid. Hospitals often have income-based repayment plans or assistance programs.

- Use an adjusted budget. While paying down debt, build a "bare-bones" budget that still allows room for occasional self-care or joy. Debt payoff should not feel like punishment.

Staying Motivated Over the Long Haul

Debt payoff can take months or years. Staying motivated requires mental stamina and regular reminders of your why.

Tips for staying the course:

- Track your progress visually. Use charts, debt trackers, or apps to see your balances shrinking.

- Celebrate milestones. Each paid-off debt is a victory. Honor it—cheaply but meaningfully.

- Find community. Online forums, financial podcasts, or social media groups can help you feel less alone.

Remind yourself: You are not your debt. Shame has no place in financial recovery.

When Bankruptcy or Settlement May Be Right

Sometimes, despite your best efforts, the numbers just don't work. You may be in a situation where your debt is unmanageable.

That's when it's time to consider alternatives.

Debt Settlement involves negotiating with creditors to pay less than you owe. It can hurt your credit short-term but may allow for a fresh start. Be cautious of for-profit companies; some nonprofits can assist with this.

Bankruptcy is a legal process that can discharge or restructure certain debts. It's a serious step, but not a moral failure. For some, it's the only path to stability.

Ask yourself:

1. Am I using most of my income just to make minimum payments?
2. Have I exhausted budgeting, side hustles, and downsizing?
3. Is debt affecting my mental or physical health?

If the answer is yes, it may be time to consult a nonprofit credit counselor or bankruptcy attorney to explore your options.

Final Thoughts

Getting out of debt isn't just about money—it's about reclaiming your future.

It's an act of healing, resilience, and empowerment. No matter where you start, the fact that you're choosing to face it means you're already moving in the right direction.

Choose a strategy that works for you, stay consistent, and remember: progress is progress, even when it's slow.

✎ Reflection | Affirmation | Prayer | Action

Debt Payoff Strategies

"Debt can feel like a heavy weight, but it's a challenge—not a sentence."

Reflection

Debt can be overwhelming and discouraging, especially when it's linked to hard times or unexpected medical bills. Yet, it doesn't define who you are or your future.

Take a moment to reflect:

1. How does your debt affect your peace of mind right now?
2. What motivates you to become debt-free?
3. Which payoff strategy—snowball or avalanche—feels more aligned with your personality and situation?
4. Are you treating yourself with grace as you work toward financial freedom?

Affirmation

I am more than my debt. Each payment I make brings me closer to freedom. I have the strength and wisdom to choose a plan that fits me. Progress, no matter how small, is victory.

Prayer

Lord, in moments when debt feels heavy and hope feels distant, remind me of Your faithfulness.

Give me patience and persistence to stay on the path You have set for me. Help me to treat myself with kindness and to celebrate every step forward.

Provide me with clarity and resources to manage my debts wisely, and guide me toward financial peace. Amen.

Action

- Choose either the Snowball or Avalanche method to begin your debt payoff journey— write down why this method suits you.
- Create a simple debt tracker (chart, spreadsheet, or app) and update it with your current balances.
- Call one medical provider or billing office to ask about payment plans or financial assistance options.
- Identify one small self-care treat you will allow yourself as a reward for reaching your next debt milestone.
- Join a supportive community online or locally (a forum, Facebook group, or podcast) to stay encouraged.

Chapter 13: Repairing your credit

Repairing your credit, especially if youre like me with multiple negative marks like repossession, charge-offs, and collections, is a challenge, but it's definitely doable with some focus and strategy.

It will take time, but here are steps you can take to see improvement faster and start rebuilding:

1. Get Your Credit Report and Dispute Errors

- Request a free copy of your credit report from all three major bureaus (Equifax, Experian, and TransUnion) at AnnualCreditReport.com. Look for any errors or inaccurate information. If you find discrepancies (like accounts that aren't yours, wrong balances, or outdated information), dispute them with the credit bureau.
- Dispute any negative items that may be incorrect to clean up your credit as much as possible.

2. Negotiate With Creditors and Collection Agencies

- Settle or negotiate: For collections accounts, try negotiating a pay-for-delete agreement. This means you pay a reduced amount (often less than the full balance), and in exchange, the collection agency agrees to remove the account from your credit report.

- Ask for goodwill adjustments: For charge-offs or accounts that are a few years old, contact the creditor directly and ask if they'd consider removing the negative mark out of goodwill, especially if you've paid the debt in full or have had a generally positive relationship with them in the past.

3. Pay Down Over-Limit Credit Cards

- Contact your creditors: If your cards are over the limit, contact the credit card issuers to negotiate a payment plan. Paying them down as quickly as possible will help reduce your credit utilization ratio, which makes up about 30% of your score.
- Focus on high-interest debt: Paying off high-interest credit cards first will save you money in the long run. As you pay down your balances, your credit utilization (the amount of credit you're using vs. your available credit) will improve, which is a significant factor in your score.

4. Settle Your Repossession

- Negotiate with the lender: If the vehicle repossession is still showing as unresolved, contact the lender. If the debt is still outstanding, you may be able to negotiate a settlement for less than the owed amount. Once settled, ask them to remove the repossession from your report.

- If the repossession was sold at auction, ensure that the remaining balance (deficiency) is reported correctly. You may be able to negotiate a lower payment.

5. Address Your Student Loans

- Income-driven repayment plans: If your student loans are federal, you can apply for an Income-Driven Repayment (IDR) plan, which bases your monthly payments on your income. This can lower your payments and prevent missed payments from harming your credit.
- If they're in default, you might be eligible for a rehabilitation program, which could remove the default status after you've made a set number of on-time payments.

Consider consolidating or refinancing your loans if you can qualify for lower payments.

6. Use a Secured Credit Card

- To rebuild credit, you can apply for a secured credit card. You deposit an amount equal to your credit limit, and the card functions just like a regular credit card. Make sure to use it responsibly (low balance and full payments on time) to build a positive credit history.

Use the card sparingly and pay it off in full each month to improve your credit utilization ratio.

7. Avoid Late Payments

- Make all payments on time moving forward. Payment history makes up 35% of your credit score. Setting up automatic payments or reminders can help you avoid missed payments.

If you can't afford full payments, make minimum payments to avoid delinquencies and late fees.

8. Keep Credit Utilization Below 30%

- Try to keep your credit card balances under 30% of your available credit. If you're carrying high balances, paying down those balances or increasing your credit limit can help reduce your utilization and boost your score.

9. Monitor Your Progress

- Use tools like Credit Karma, Experian, or Mint to track your credit score over time and see how your efforts are paying off. It can be motivating to see gradual improvements, even if small at first.

10. Consider Credit Counseling or a Debt Management Plan (DMP)

- If you're feeling overwhelmed by multiple debts and collections, seeking help from a nonprofit credit counseling agency can be beneficial. They may help you create a debt repayment plan and even negotiate with creditors on your behalf.

Be Patient, but Persistent

Repairing credit doesn't happen overnight, but with consistent effort, you should start to see improvements in 3-6 months, especially as you pay down debt and make payments on time.

The key is to address as much of the negative information as possible and rebuild your credit by managing your remaining debts responsibly.

꧁ Reflection | Affirmation | Prayer | Action

Repairing Your Credit

"Repairing credit is challenging but doable with focus and strategy."

Reflection

Credit issues can feel discouraging, especially when multiple negative marks weigh you down. Take a moment to reflect:

1. What emotions come up when you think about your credit report?
2. How has poor credit affected your life or opportunities?
3. What small steps can you commit to that would start improving your credit?
4. How can you show yourself patience and kindness during this journey?

Affirmation

I am capable of rebuilding my credit and restoring my financial health. Every step I take toward repairing my credit is progress. I choose persistence over perfection and grace over guilt.

Prayer

God, give me the wisdom to navigate the complexities of credit repair.

Help me to be diligent, patient, and honest with myself as I work toward healing my financial future.

Grant me peace in moments of frustration, and guide me to resources and support that will help me succeed. Amen.

Action

- Request your free credit reports from Equifax, Experian, and TransUnion at AnnualCreditReport.com. Review carefully for errors and file disputes on any inaccuracies.
- Reach out to one creditor or collection agency to negotiate a pay-for-delete or goodwill adjustment.
- Make a plan to pay down one over-limit credit card, prioritizing those with the highest interest
- Explore applying for a secured credit card to begin rebuilding positive credit history.
- Set up automatic payments or reminders to avoid future late payments.
- Track your credit progress monthly using a free tool like Credit Karma or Experian.
- If overwhelmed, research nonprofit credit counseling agencies in your area for additional support.

Part IV: Growing Financial Stability

Breaking the Paycheck-to-Paycheck Cycle

Understand why it's especially challenging to break this cycle with chronic illness and explore strategies to build buffers and live one month ahead. Also included are gentle side hustle ideas tailored to your energy levels.

Chapter 14: Building Emergency Funds & Savings

Saving might feel out of reach—especially if you've spent years just trying to stay afloat.

But saving isn't just for the wealthy or the lucky. It's a tool for reclaiming control. Whether you're putting away coins in a jar or setting up automatic transfers, every step is a step toward freedom.

In this chapter, we'll walk through how to build an emergency fund from scratch, set up savings goals (even small ones), and start dreaming beyond survival. Even if all you have is $5—that's enough to begin.

How to Save Even When It Feels Impossible

Let's be honest: when bills are stacking up and income is stretched thin, saving can feel like a luxury. But savings—even small ones—are your financial buffer. They protect you from going further into debt when life throws something unexpected your way.

Start with these foundational principles:

- Define your "why." Knowing why you're saving gives it meaning—whether it's avoiding payday loans, covering a car repair, or buying breathing room.

- Start small, stay consistent. Try $5 a week. Or $1 a day. The amount matters less than the habit.
- Make it automatic. If possible, set up auto-transfers to savings on payday. You won't miss what you never see.

No amount is too small. Progress isn't measured in thousands of dollars—it's measured in intention and repetition.

Emergency Funds: Your Financial Life Vest

An emergency fund isn't about fear—it's about freedom. It keeps a flat tire or a lost job from turning into a crisis.

1. How much do you need?

Starter goal: $500–$1,000. Enough for basic unexpected expenses.

Long-term goal: 3–6 months of essential expenses. It takes time—don't rush.

2. Where should you keep it?

In a separate savings account, ideally at a bank you don't check daily.

Avoid investing it—this money needs to be accessible, not at risk.

3. **How to build it:**
   - Use windfalls (tax refunds, bonuses, cash gifts).
   - Sell unused items or put side hustle income toward it.
   - Cut one small expense and redirect it to savings.
   - Micro-Saving and Side Hustles

If you're living paycheck to paycheck, you may need creative strategies to find money to save.

Try micro-saving tactics:

1. Round-up apps that save the change from purchases.
2. "No spend" days or weeks—track how much you save.
3. Envelope systems or digital equivalents to physically set money aside.

Consider low-barrier side hustles:

- Gig apps (deliveries, surveys, errands).
- Selling secondhand items online.
- Freelancing a skill or offering a service in your community.

Even an extra $50/month can jump-start your savings and boost your confidence.

Sinking Funds: Planning for the Predictable

Not all expenses are emergencies. Some come every year—like holidays, birthdays, or car maintenance. That's where sinking funds come in.

A **sinking fund** is a mini-savings account for a specific, known expense.

You set aside a little each month so you're ready when the time comes.

Examples:

$30/month for Christmas = $360 by December.

$20/month for vet bills or kids' clothes.

$10/week for future travel—dreams matter too.

You don't have to dread these expenses anymore. You'll be prepared—and proud.

Building Wealth Slowly and Steadily

Wealth isn't just about six figures and stocks. It's about ownership, options, and peace of mind. And it's built one choice at a time.

Here's how to start building wealth even on a tight budget:

1. Pay yourself first. Even if it's $10 per paycheck.
2. Avoid high-interest debt. Paying off debt is a form of saving.

3. Learn about compound interest. Over time, money you save or invest starts working for you.

Most importantly: Don't compare your chapter 1 to someone else's chapter 20. Your pace is your power.

Saving isn't just a financial act— it's an emotional one. It tells the world (and yourself) that you believe in tomorrow.

It says: "I am worth preparing for."

Whether you're putting away $1 or $100, you are laying the foundation for security, stability, and possibility.

Start where you are. Use what you have. And never stop dreaming bigger.

🪶 Reflection | Affirmation | Prayer | Action

Building Emergency Funds and Saving Goals

"Saving is a tool for reclaiming control—even when it feels impossible."

Reflection

Saving money can feel overwhelming when you're used to just making it through the day. Reflect on:

1. What does having a financial safety net mean to you emotionally and practically?
2. What fears or barriers keep you from saving right now?
3. How might even a small amount saved regularly change your sense of security?
4. What is your personal "why" for saving? How does that purpose motivate you?

Affirmation

I am capable of building financial stability, one small step at a time. Every dollar I save is an investment in my peace of mind and future freedom. I honor my progress and trust the process.

Prayer

God, please give me the patience and discipline to build my savings, even when it feels hard.

Help me to trust that small, consistent actions matter and that You are with me on this journey.

Teach me to be wise and hopeful as I prepare for whatever comes next. Amen.

Action

- Define your personal reason for saving—write down your "why."
- Start a savings habit by setting aside a small amount (even $1 or $5) weekly or monthly.
- Open a separate savings account or use a dedicated envelope for your emergency fund.
- Use any windfalls or extra income (tax refunds, side hustle earnings) to boost your savings.
- Try a micro-saving technique like round-up apps or "no spend" days to find extra money.
- Set up sinking funds for predictable expenses (holidays, birthdays, car repairs) with small monthly contributions.
- Learn about compound interest and commit to "paying yourself first" by saving before spending.

Chapter 15: Planning for the Future

You deserve more than survival—you deserve stability, dignity, and the freedom to dream beyond the next crisis.

Planning might feel like a luxury when you've been stuck in fight-or-flight mode for years. But it's not just for the wealthy or worry-free. It's for you, too.

In this chapter, we'll walk through gentle, realistic steps to start securing your future:

from basic estate planning and guardianship, to low-effort income ideas that honor your energy, to building a version of financial freedom that actually works for your life.

This is your invitation to think long-term—and to know you're worth planning for.

Estate Planning and Guardianship: Protecting What Matters

Estate planning sounds intimidating, but at its core, it's about protecting your people and having a say in what happens—no matter your income or assets.

What is estate planning?

It's simply making legal decisions about:

- Who will care for your children or dependents if you can't.
- What happens to your belongings (yes, even if you don't "own" much).
- Who makes medical and financial decisions for you if you're unable.

Start with these basics:

1. Name a guardian for your children in a legally valid will. This is one of the most powerful and loving things you can do.
2. Create a simple will. Many online tools or nonprofit legal clinics can help you for free or low-cost.
3. Set up a health care proxy and power of attorney. These let someone you trust step in during a medical emergency.

You don't need a lawyer to get started—but you do need a plan.

Planning isn't about being morbid.

It's about peace of mind.

Passive Income Ideas for Moms with Limited Energy

When your days are full and your energy is low, the idea of side hustles can feel exhausting. But passive income—money that trickles in with minimal effort—can help ease the pressure without burning you out.

Here are some gentle, realistic ideas:

- Print-on-demand shops (like Etsy or Redbubble): Create simple digital designs (quotes, patterns, art) once, and earn income over time.
- Affiliate links or blogging: If you already share tips, products, or parenting wisdom online, turn those into small commissions.
- Sell digital downloads: Budget templates, meal planners, or self-care checklists—simple tools that help others.
- Write an eBook or guide: You've lived through a lot—your knowledge is valuable.

Even if you make $20/month to start, it's a seed. Passive income grows slowly, but it can grow. The key is choosing something aligned with your strengths, not your stress.

Finding Financial Freedom on Your Own Terms

Financial freedom isn't just about being rich. It's about having choices—and not being ruled by fear, bills, or burnout.

Ask yourself:

1. What does freedom look like to me?
2. Is it fewer hours at work? A safe home? No longer dreading the mailbox?
3. Is it the ability to say "yes" to your kids, or "no" to a toxic situation?

Freedom starts with small wins:

- An emergency fund.
- A budget that includes joy, not just survival.
- A plan that reflects your values—not someone else's timeline.

You don't have to hustle your way to wealth. You can build freedom slowly, with intention, rest, and resilience.

Planning for the future doesn't mean you have to have all the answers—it just means you believe you have a future. That belief alone is a radical act of self-worth.

You are worthy of peace, preparation, and possibility. You are allowed to think ahead—not because everything is perfect, but because you are growing beyond survival.

Whether you're writing a will, starting a side income stream, or just dreaming again, you're planting seeds of hope.

This isn't just about money—it's about legacy.

And you are building one, right now.

🐾 Reflection | Affirmation | Prayer | Action

Planning for the Future

"You deserve stability, dignity, and the freedom to dream beyond survival."

Reflection

Take a moment to reflect on your future and legacy:

1. What does financial freedom and security look like for you personally?
2. How might planning ahead bring you peace of mind today?
3. What fears or doubts come up when you think about estate planning or long-term money goals?
4. How can small steps toward passive income or legal planning honor your current energy and life situation?

Affirmation

I am worthy of planning for my future and protecting those I love. Each small action I take today plants seeds for a life of freedom, choice, and peace. I move forward with courage, rest, and intention.

Prayer

God, grant me wisdom and strength to prepare for tomorrow with hope and confidence.

Help me to care for my family through practical steps, and to trust that You are guiding me toward a future filled with peace and possibility. Amen.

Action

- Begin or review your estate planning by naming a guardian, creating a simple will, and setting up a health care proxy or power of attorney.
- Research free or low-cost legal resources or online tools to make this easier.
- Explore one passive income idea that fits your interests and energy level (print-on-demand, digital downloads, affiliate links, writing).
- Reflect on what financial freedom means to you and write down 2–3 small goals that move you toward that vision.
- Keep your financial plan aligned with your values and allow yourself to build freedom gradually, with grace.

Chapter 16: 5 Steps to Start Your Estate Plan

Because your voice matters—even when you're not there to speak.

Here's a simple and empowering "5 Steps to Start Your Estate Plan" checklist.

1. **Name a Guardian for Your Children**
   - Decide who you trust to care for your children if something happens to you.
   - Have a conversation with them to confirm they're willing and able.
   - Put it in writing—this can be included in a simple will.

2. **Create a Basic Will**
   - Outline who should receive your belongings, even if they're few.
   - Name an executor (someone you trust to carry out your wishes).
   - Use a free or low-cost legal aid site if needed (many are state-specific).

3. **Assign a Health Care Proxy**
   - Choose someone to make medical decisions for you if you're unable to.
   - Discuss your values and wishes for healthcare and life support.

- Fill out a legally valid form—usually available through your state or local health department.

4. **Set Up a Financial Power of Attorney**
   - This gives someone you trust the authority to manage your finances in an emergency.
   - Make sure it's someone financially responsible and aligned with your values.
   - You can make it temporary, limited, or long-term.

5. **Store and Share Your Documents**
   - Keep your will and forms in a safe but accessible place.
   - Give copies or instructions to a trusted person.

Write down account passwords, insurance info, and other key contacts.

Bonus Tip:

Revisit your plan once a year—or after any big life change (a move, new child, marriage/divorce, or major health shift).

✿ Reflection | Affirmation | Prayer | Action

5 Steps to Start Your Estate Plan

"Your voice matters—even when you're not there to speak."

Reflection

Consider the peace that comes from knowing your loved ones will be cared for, no matter what happens.

1. Who are the people you trust most to look after your children and decisions?
2. How does taking these simple steps empower you and bring peace to your family?
3. What feelings come up when you think about putting your wishes into writing?

Affirmation

I am taking brave and loving steps to protect my family's future.

My voice matters, and my plans today will bring security and peace tomorrow.

I am capable of creating a legacy of care and responsibility.

Prayer

Lord, guide me as I take these important steps to protect my family.

Give me clarity and courage to make decisions that honor my values and care deeply for those I love.

Help me to trust in Your provision and peace throughout this process. Amen.

Action

- Choose and talk with a guardian for your children—ensure they are willing and able.
- Create a basic will, using free or low-cost resources if needed.
- Assign a health care proxy and discuss your medical wishes openly.
- Set up a financial power of attorney with someone trustworthy and responsible.
- Store all documents safely and share instructions with a trusted person.
- Schedule an annual review of your estate plan or revisit it after any major life changes.

Chapter 17: Real Stories from Moms Who Did It

You are not alone.

In this chapter, you'll meet other single moms with chronic illness who took control of their finances one step at a time. Their stories will inspire and remind you that progress—not perfection—is what matters.

My Testimony

If anybody can tell you "I can," it's me.

I went from minimum wage and renting an apartment to making close to five figures a month in a two-income family. We just purchased a house and started renovations. I drove a brand-new 2019 Kia Sorento with third row seating and he a 2016 Yukon XL, Ram 1500 Big Horn and a boat.

I homeschooled the kids and thought I was building a future with my so-called husband. I just got certified in my field and was hired in my dream department.

I just started my nursing/surgical technician program, which would keep me busy during the day, I continued working my full-time night position. I planned our first-ever family vacation and put it on my credit cards, believing I would have the money to pay it back later.

Boy, was I wrong.

After returning from the trip, I became extremely sick. After a long hospital stay, I was unable to return to work and started receiving short-term disability benefits, which were only 60% of my pay.

Believing I would soon qualify for long-term disability and SSDI (Social Security Disability Insurance), I continued charging my credit cards to make up for the lost income.

During this time, my then-not-husband was checking out on us as a family, and I eventually had to let him go. He became a liability. I could no longer absorb the impact of his poor decisions—they were killing our family and killing me.

So with that, I lost his income as well.

Here I am now, living on less than 150% of my previous income but carrying 200% of the debt—if that makes sense.

I have the house and the kids for sure, but I also have all the debt accumulated over the years. Why? Because over the course of our fifteen-year relationship, I was the credit, and he was the income.

We qualified together, but my name was always primary on the things that mattered—except the Yukon XL. I could never get behind that purchase, and I knew better than to cosign—thank you, Jesus, I wasn't too dumb; I had some sense.

I'm kidding, but seriously.

I may play dumb, deaf, or blind sometimes, but I ain't never played stupid. And you can quote me on that!

Moving forward:

Here we are, barely able to pay bills and afford groceries. Door-dashing meals because, during this time, I also had two surgeries: a port surgery to implant my Bard port for treatments and a knee surgery.

During an intense argument with my not-ex-husband, I slipped and tore some stuff in my knee. Please don't ask me how I got upset with myself. No, he didn't do it directly, but he was fully the cause.

Moving on, anyway.

I was new at receiving treatments—infusions and blood exchanges—and still on crutches attending physical therapy.

Cooking wasn't a huge option for me, and my not-ex-husband had to work and bar hop with his friends and girlfriends, so he didn't have time to cook or help me out.

Believing that I would receive a lump sum soon, I kept charging because what else could I do?

I had great credit—well over 720—and was definitely about to hit my goal of 750 because I had access to his income to pay the debt. I had a system set up to maximize my credit score for the best rates and limits.

I would charge everything: bills, groceries, gas, etc. If they took credit, I paid credit. I would then turn around and pay the card's balance normally to zero.

Doing this over time showed creditors I was trustworthy to lend to, so my limits were constantly increased, and I could apply for low-interest personal loans.

With our combined income and my Suze Orman/Dave Ramsey skills, I was on a mission. Our family was going to be rich.

So here I am charging and charging on these high-limit cards, believing one day I could stop charging and start paying back more than the minimum once I received my SSDI back pay for all the months that had passed since my application.

Y'all, it took them almost two years to approve my claim. My back pay and monthly amount were only a fraction of what I anticipated and budgeted.

Talk about more stress.

What they gave me wasn't enough to get out of the hole I was in, and the monthly amount wouldn't be enough to carry me forward. I still haven't received any of the financial support that was promised.

It took me some time to realize no one was coming to save me. Money wasn't going to fall from the sky, no matter how much I prayed. And baby mama, I WAS PRAYING.

Father God, You know what I need. You know what I want. Please, please, please.

No, but for real.

What else can you do with hungry mouths and red delinquency notices everywhere? You start praying, maybe crying, but for sure praying. After that, you start planning. How do I get there from here with what I have here?

It's called building blocks. You can't go upstairs without taking one step at a time. You are down here, and you're trying to go up there. Step by step, day by day.

It took fifteen years for me, my ex-not-husband, our four children, our three dogs, two new trucks, and a new house for me to get in the financial hole I'm in right now. It's not magically going to be gone tomorrow.

Just like the mess took time to be created, the cleanup might take just as long.

That's not to discourage you—that's just to say get started sooner so you can hurry up and get to the finish line, because it's so possible to be financially free. It's not pretty, but it is possible.

📖 Reflection | Affirmation | Prayer | Action

Real Stories from Moms Who Did It

Reflection

Think about your own journey and the obstacles you've faced.

1. What lessons can you take from the story of resilience and persistence shared here?
2. How does hearing someone else's truth encourage you to keep moving forward?

Affirmation

I am capable of overcoming my financial challenges one step at a time. My story is still being written, and each day I make progress. I honor my strength and resilience.

Prayer

Dear God, thank You for the courage to keep going, even when the road is hard.

Please give me strength, wisdom, and peace as I work to rebuild and create a stable future for my family.

Help me to trust the process and to celebrate each small victory. Amen.

Action

- Identify one small financial step you can take today toward stability.
- Reach out for support from a trusted friend, mentor, or community group when you feel overwhelmed.
- Keep a journal to track your progress and remind yourself how far you've come.
- Celebrate small wins—no matter how tiny— they build momentum.

Chapter 18: Staying Motivated

There will be hard days.

Days when the budget feels tight, progress feels slow, or life throws another unexpected challenge your way. But remember this: your why is stronger.

You're not just budgeting—you're building something beautiful. For yourself. For your children. For your future. Staying motivated isn't about perfection. It's about perspective, progress, and giving yourself credit for every step forward.

Celebrate the Wins

Every milestone matters.

- Paid off a credit card?
- Built your first $500 emergency fund?
- Made it through a month sticking to your zero-based budget?

Celebrate it. Not just with words—but with intention. A small treat. A moment of reflection. A smile in the mirror.

Celebrating your wins reinforces positive habits and keeps you motivated. It's not about big rewards, but about recognizing your effort and reminding yourself that you're doing it—and it's working.

Reflect on What's Working

Zero-based budgeting isn't just about numbers—it's about clarity and control. Look back at how far you've come and what helped you get there. Was it sticking to your budget? Tracking every dollar? Saying no when it mattered?

Then: Set new goals.

- Build a bigger emergency fund.
- Start saving for a family trip.
- Begin investing for the future.

Revisit your budget and adjust it to match your new priorities. You're growing—and your budget should grow with you.

Find or Create a Supportive Community

You don't have to do this alone.

Whether it's online groups, financial accountability buddies, or just one friend who cheers you on— community matters. Find people who understand your journey and celebrate your growth.

Benefits of Support:

- Financial awareness: You know exactly where every dollar is going.
- Intentional spending: You're aligning your choices with your values.
- Debt reduction and savings: You're prioritizing what matters most.

Challenges to Watch For:

- Time commitment: Budgeting takes attention and regular check-ins.
- Discipline: Especially with variable income or fluctuating expenses, it can be tough to stick to a plan.

But here's the truth: zero-based budgeting gives you power. You're telling your money where to go, instead of wondering where it went. It keeps you focused on your needs, your goals, and your future.

Budgeting Is Freedom, Not Restriction

Let's be clear: budgeting isn't about punishment—it's about possibility. It's about giving every dollar a job, so your money works for you, not against you.

Yes, it takes discipline. But once you get the hang of it, your finances will feel less chaotic and more peaceful. You'll start to feel in control—and that's worth celebrating, too.

Quick Tips to Stay on Track

1. Start small. Don't try to fix everything at once. Begin with savings and debt, and slowly refine your discretionary spending.
2. Cover the basics first. Make sure your essentials—housing, food, utilities—are protected before anything else.
3. Tweak your budget monthly. Life changes. Your budget should, too.
4. Give yourself grace. You won't do this perfectly every time. That's okay.

You did it—and you'll keep doing it. Your progress is real, your effort is powerful, and your story is just beginning.

This journey isn't just about dollars and cents. It's about freedom, stability, and legacy. It's about showing your kids what resilience looks like. And when people see what you've done, they'll know they can do it too.

You're building something beautiful.

You're doing a great job.

And I'm proud of you.

🦋 Reflection | Affirmation | Prayer | Action

Staying Motivated

Reflection

1. What motivates you to keep going, even on tough days? Reflect on the progress you've made so far and the vision you have for your future.
2. How can you honor yourself for every step, no matter how small?

Affirmation

I celebrate every win, learn from every challenge, and keep moving forward with strength and grace. My journey is unique, and I am proud of my progress.

Prayer

God, thank You for walking with me on this journey.

Help me to stay motivated and hopeful when times get hard.

Remind me that every small step is part of Your bigger plan for my life.

Give me peace, patience, and perseverance as I build a better future. Amen.

Action

- Take a moment today to celebrate one recent win, no matter the size.
- Reach out to someone who supports your goals and share your progress.
- Write down one new financial goal or intention for the next month.
- Practice self-compassion when things don't go perfectly.

Scriptures for Stewardship & Discipline

Proverbs 21:20 (NLT)

The wise have wealth and luxury, but fools spend whatever they get.

Luke 16:10 (NLT)

Whoever is faithful with little is also faithful with much.

1 Corinthians 4:2 (NLT)

It is required that those who have been given a trust must prove faithful.

Proverbs 3:9-10 (NLT)

Honor the Lord with your wealth, with the firstfruits of all your crops; then your barns will be filled with plenty.

Closing Prayer:

- Lord, give me wisdom and discipline to manage my resources well. Help me honor You with every financial decision I make.

Book Club / Group Discussion Questions

The questions are thoughtfully balanced to encourage reflection, sharing, and actionable insights, with a focus on core themes of faith, chronic illness, budgeting, and legacy.

General Reflection

1. Which chapter impacted you the most — and why?
2. How did your understanding of wealth and legacy shift after going through this workbook?
3. What limiting beliefs about money or legacy did you identify in yourself? How are you working to overcome them?
4. What step or strategy in the book felt the most empowering or doable for you?
5. How can we support one another in staying accountable to our legacy and financial goals?
6. What is one thing you want your children or loved ones to remember about how you built your life?
7. How has your faith influenced your view of wealth-building and financial stewardship?
8. What does faith-based wealth building look like in your family now?
9. What's your next financial or legacy-related step after reading this book?

Personal Connection & Challenges

10. Which part of Shaundra's financial journey did you relate to the most—and why?
11. How does living with chronic illness affect your ability to budget, earn, or save? What are some unique challenges you face?
12. What fears, doubts, or beliefs around money have you carried? How did this workbook challenge or change those?
13. How do you balance medical costs and day-to-day living expenses in your household?
14. What's your biggest struggle with staying consistent in your budgeting or financial routine?

Practical Application

15. Which budgeting tool, tip, or habit from the workbook are you most excited to try or have already tried?
16. How does zero-based budgeting help you "tell every dollar where to go"?
17. Have you tried or are you interested in cash envelope stuffing? What questions or concerns do you still have?
18. How can budgeting become a form of self-care, especially for moms managing chronic illness or solo parenting?
19. What's one financial habit you plan to change or implement moving forward?

20. What side hustle or micro-saving idea from the book feels most accessible for your current energy and lifestyle?

Looking Forward & Encouragement

21. What does "financial breakthrough" mean to you—and what is your next step toward it?
22. If you could share one chapter or lesson from the workbook with another mom who's struggling financially, which would it be—and why?
23. How has this workbook changed your mindset about money, scarcity, and abundance?
24. What role does community and support play in your financial journey? How can you build or strengthen that support?
25. What is your vision for your family's financial legacy? How will you start building it today?

Glossary

A quick reference guide to financial, faith, and mindset terms used throughout this book. Designed to bring clarity, confidence, and calm as you build your legacy.

Financial & Budgeting Terms (A–Z)

Action Plan — A clear set of small, doable steps toward your financial goals.

Affirmation — A positive, faith-based statement that strengthens your mindset and focus.

Automated Savings — A system that transfers money from checking to savings automatically.

Buffer Fund — A small cushion to prevent overdrafts or cover minor surprises.

Budget — A plan for how you'll spend, save, and give each dollar. A roadmap to peace, not pressure.

Budget Categories — The specific areas you assign your money to, like groceries or rent.

Cash Envelope System — A budgeting method using labeled envelopes for cash spending.

Cash Stuffing — Physically adding money into envelopes or binders for set categories.

Chronic Illness — A long-term health condition requiring ongoing care and adaptability.

Debt Avalanche — Paying off debts starting with the highest interest rate to save money long-term.

Debt Snowball — Paying off smallest debts first for motivation and quick wins.

Emergency Fund — Money set aside for true emergencies—medical crises, job loss, repairs.

Estate Plan — Legal documents that protect your children, assets, and medical wishes.

Faith-Based Stewardship — Managing your finances with purpose, gratitude, and trust in God.

Financial Clarity — Knowing where your money comes from, where it goes, and why.

Financial Legacy — What you build and leave behind for future generations.

Fixed Expenses — Bills that stay the same each month (rent, insurance).

Flexible Expenses — Variable costs that change monthly (groceries, gas).

Grace-Driven Habits — Progress over perfection; choosing consistency over guilt.

Income — The money you earn or receive regularly.

Living with Intention — Spending and saving in alignment with your faith and values.

Medical Expenses — Health-related costs for care, treatment, and medication.

Mindset Shift — Changing how you think about money—from scarcity to abundance.

Net Income — What you actually take home after taxes and deductions.

Non-Negotiables — Essential expenses or priorities that support your values.

Passive Income — Money earned with little ongoing effort (interest, royalties).

Reflection — Taking time to review, learn, and celebrate progress.

Sinking Fund — Savings for non-monthly expenses (birthdays, car repairs, holidays).

Stewardship — Managing what's in your hands—time, money, energy—with care and wisdom.

Surplus — The money left after budgeting your monthly needs.

Tithe — Giving a portion (traditionally 10%) of income back to God through your church or community.

Variable Income — Income that changes each month (gig work, freelance, disability payments).

Wealth-Building — Growing stability and assets for your future and family.

Zero-Based Budgeting — Giving every dollar a purpose so that income minus expenses equals zero.

Faith & Mindset Terms (A-Z)

Abundance Mindset — Believing there's enough for you and others; rooted in trust, not fear.

Breakthrough — A moment when prayer, strategy, and perseverance align to move you forward.

Divine Provision — God's faithful supply of your needs in both ordinary and miraculous ways.

Faith Stewardship — Managing your resources in obedience and gratitude to God.

Financial Healing — Restoring peace and confidence in how you view and handle money.

Grace Over Grind — Choosing peace, pacing, and divine timing over burnout and hustle.

Kingdom Wealth — Wealth used for purpose and service, not status.

Legacy Mindset — Thinking generationally—building systems and habits that bless your children's future.

Purpose-Driven Prosperity — Aligning your financial goals with your calling and values.

Restorative Faith — Choosing to believe again after disappointment or hardship.

Seed — Anything you give or plant in faith, expecting God to bring increase.

Stewardship Over Striving — Focusing on faithful management instead of control or fear.

Testimony — Your personal story of God's faithfulness through challenges and change.

Vision — The God-given picture of your future that directs your steps and financial goals.

Wealth with Purpose — Using money to create impact, legacy, and freedom—not just comfort.

Remember: Every term you learn, every step you take, and every prayer you whisper is part of your healing journey. You are building more than wealth—you are building legacy.

Resources

Your journey doesn't end with the last chapter—
these tools and guides can help you stay supported,
informed, and inspired. Whether you're just starting
or already making progress, these resources are here
to remind you: you are not alone.

Budgeting Templates available for download at
www.warriormomacademy.com

Simple tools to make your money easier to manage

- Zero-Based Budget Worksheet – Allocate
  every dollar to a purpose before the month
  begins.

- Monthly Budget Template – Track income,
  fixed expenses, variable expenses, and
  savings goals.

- Sinking Fund Tracker – Plan ahead for non-
  monthly expenses like holidays, car repairs,
  or school supplies.

- Emergency Fund Tracker – Watch your
  progress grow with a visual savings
  thermometer or checklist.
  (You can create or customize these using free
  tools like Google Sheets, Notion, or printable
  PDFs from budget blogs and apps.)

List of Assistance Programs

You don't have to do everything on your own. These programs can help with essentials while you rebuild.

National Programs (U.S.):

- SNAP (Supplemental Nutrition Assistance Program) – Food assistance based on income.

- WIC (Women, Infants, and Children) – Nutrition support for mothers and young children.

- LIHEAP – Help with heating and energy bills.

- Medicaid/CHIP – Healthcare for low-income families and individuals.

- Section 8 & Housing Choice Vouchers – Subsidized housing assistance.

- TANF (Temporary Assistance for Needy Families) – Cash aid and job support for families in need.

Additional Support:
- 211.org – Find local help for food, housing, healthcare, and utilities.

- Modest Needs Foundation – Offers short-term emergency grants for unexpected expenses.

- Single Moms Planet – Community and financial support specifically for single mothers.

Books, Podcasts, and YouTube Channels

For education, motivation, and community

Books:

- "The Total Money Makeover" by Dave Ramsey – Classic guide to debt payoff and budgeting (take what works, leave what doesn't).
- "Your Money or Your Life" by Vicki Robin – A mindful, values-based approach to money.
- "Broke Millennial" by Erin Lowry – Great for beginners or those starting over.

Podcasts:

- The Clever Girls Know Podcast – Real stories and practical tips from women changing their financial futures.
- Afford Anything – Focuses on making smarter decisions about money, time, and energy.

- Frugal Friends Podcast – Encouraging and humorous look at budgeting, frugality, and intentional spending.

YouTube Channels:

- The Budget Mom – Practical zero-based budgeting advice and real-life examples.
- One Big Happy Life – Focused on financial independence and long-term planning for families.
- Tasha Talks Finance – Accessible content on budgeting, saving, and financial mindset.

Chronic Illness-Friendly Budget Tools

Because your energy matters just as much as your income

- YNAB (You Need a Budget) – A flexible app that allows for unpredictable income and medical expenses. Great for pacing.

- Goodbudget – Envelope-style budgeting for people who like a simple, low-energy system.

- Tiller Money – Automated spreadsheets for those who want control without manual entry.

- Google Sheets Templates – Free, customizable, and can be updated slowly—no rush, no pressure.

Tips for Budgeting with Low Energy:

- Set up automated savings and bill pay where possible.

- Budget in short, timed sessions (try 10–15 minute intervals).

- Use voice-to-text apps or budgeting via mobile if typing is difficult.
  Don't strive for perfection—aim for progress.

The Warrior Mom's Guide™ Book Series

FOUNDATION: The Pilot Book

🤍 A Warrior Within, A Chronic Illness

The Warrior Mom's Guide to Sickle Cell & Chronic Resilience

My story of battling sickle cell while raising a family—woven with practical mindset shifts, survival tools, and advocacy.

📖 The heart of the Warrior Mom movement and the introduction to the series.

THE DEEP-DIVE SERIES (Books 1–10)

🤍 **The Warrior Mom's Guide to GhettoOCD™** (Home Organization & Cleaning)

Practical, real-life homemaking strategies for moms with chronic illness.

🌸 **The Warrior Mom's Guide to Mental Wellness & Finding Joy in the Chaos**

Therapy, prayer, and emotional survival tools for weary moms.

💜 **The Warrior Mom's Guide to Single Motherhood by Choice**

Reclaiming peace, health, and wholeness after carrying it all.

💜 **The Warrior Mom's Guide to Loving Unexpectedly**

Guardianship, Fostering & Adoption with Faith and Fierce Love

Finding your voice, courage, and confidence in nontraditional motherhood.

💜 **The Warrior Mom's Guide to Generational Wealth & Family Legacy**

Building wealth, purpose, and a future that lasts.

💜 **The Warrior Mom's Guide to Spiritual Reset & Chronic Faith**

Faith after diagnosis, grace during flare-ups, and spiritual renewal when you feel forgotten.

⚫ **The Warrior Mom's Guide to ZBB & Cash Stuffing** (Finances)

Zero-based budgeting & cash envelope systems for sick-day survival.

🪴 The Warrior Mom's Guide to Homeschooling for the Homegirls

Practical tools for rest, rejuvenation, and chronic-illness-friendly homeschooling.

🩶 The Warrior Mom's Guide to Homeownership & Stability

Creative paths to securing a home with chronic illness and limited income.

🌿 The Warrior Mom's Guide to Living in Peace

End-of-life planning with grace: wills, medical directives, legacy projects, and restoration.

Find the books, companion workbooks, journals, planners, and more at:

www.warriormomacademy.com

About the Author

Shaundra M. G. Harris is a writer, single mother of four, chronic illness warrior, and the heart behind The Warrior Mom Movement. As a homeschooling mama living with sickle cell disease, Shaundra understands the intersection of medical hardship, solo parenting, and financial struggle.

From surviving trauma to building stability through faith, she has developed practical, hope-filled resources to help other women not only survive—but thrive. She is the author of The Warrior Mom's Guide series, a speaker, and a passionate advocate for generational wealth, legacy-building, and grace-filled planning—even on a tight budget.

Her work blends humor, Holy Spirit, and hard-won wisdom. Through her books, online community, and real-life encouragement, Shaundra empowers women to build from what they have, believe for more, and leave a lasting legacy of strength.

▊ Follow Shaun the Mom: @warriormomacademy (Instagram, Facebook, TikTok)

⊕ Join the Thrive Hive: A community of warrior moms supporting one another.

www.warriormomacademy.com

Acknowledgments

To every mother who ever wondered if she was doing enough—this is for you.

To the women rising through illness, trauma, poverty, and pain—I see you. You are legacy in motion.

To my children—thank you for being my "why," my joy, and my motivation to keep going.

To my family, friends, and faith community—thank you for believing in me when I couldn't believe in myself.

To every sickle cell warrior, single mama, and woman budgeting on faith and grit—your strength inspires this work.

And to my Creator—all glory to You.

Thank you for walking this journey with me.

Happy Budgeting!

visit www.shaunthemom.com

or

www.warriormomacademy.com